Walking Art Practice

Reflections on Socially Engaged Paths

Ernesto Pujol

tp

Triarchy Press

Published by Triarchy Press
Axminster, England
First Edition, 2018

info@triarchypress.net
www.triarchypress.net

ISBNs:
Paperback: 978-1-911193-36-4
ePub: 978-1-911193-37-1

Cover design: Ernesto Pujol
Images from 'Speaking in Silence', Honolulu, 2011, courtesy of the artist

This book is dedicated to three unforgettable walking teachers:

Alma Pujol, my mother, in memory of our urban walks
Saralyn Reece Hardy, walker of the Kansas prairie
Rebecca Solnit, for her inspiring *Wanderlust*

> not my thoughts
> but my steps
> connect me
> with others

Preface

Walking threads thoughts triggered and pursued, then dropped and picked up to their resolution, or left by the roadside, until who knows when. This is a book about *the when.*

This is a hybrid book with art book elements and the personal content of a field journal that shares reflections by a socially engaged, cultural practitioner. It may serve as a manifesto for artists who walk and a resource for performers—a performative walking manual.

Although this book has a structure consisting of three thematic parts, I have written it in such a way that readers can open the book anywhere and read my 68 reflections in any order.

In terms of order, all walking is repetitive. Therefore, there is a certain amount of conscious overlapping and repetition because I have allowed it to be reflective of the repetitiveness of walking, of how repetitive steps work the mind of the walker.

I wish to acknowledge my friends Lori Brack and Kate Zeller for their helpful suggestions about my first manuscript. I also wish to thank all who have supported my walking art projects over the years as funders, hosts, curators, advisors, colleagues, partners, producers, performers, volunteers, docents, documentarians, journalists, and friends. My performative walks have been collective productions and experiences that would not have happened without their trust, loyalty, and generosity.

I also wish to voice the gratitude of many walkers in thanking Triarchy Press for their commitment to books on walking. I personally wish to thank my editor, Andrew Carey, for being "a word man" and reclaiming the original title of "Roadside Spiritualities," which had been *strategically* changed to "Roadside Philosophies." Andrew gently reminded me of my own beliefs: that religious rituals should not be confused with the intuitive gestures of the human spirit, which sustain our walking through creative beliefs about the road.

Contents

Introduction: *First Steps*

"The universe only winks at the ones
no one will believe."
Michael Cunningham, *The Snow Queen*

We walk. No one taught us how. We taught ourselves, while adults watched in awe, holding our hands, trying to protect us from bump, fall, and hurt. However, for most of us, that early childhood experience is beyond recall.

Unless we walk for healthy exercise or meaningful pilgrimage, technology has eliminated our need for long-distance walking. Few in the West walk to work. Most step to and from their car, bus, or train, stepping across the street, to the corner, around the block. At most, we stroll through farmers' markets, shops, and malls. The housebound, interned, and imprisoned move from room to room.

Is this truly walking? Walking erect was one of the gestures and experiences that made us human. Walking is connected to breathing; to the intake of oxygen for the brain; to the lubrication of joints; to the flow of our metabolism and digestion; and to the burning of calories. Walking keeps the body healthy, if not alive. It is a medical fact that the minute we stop moving, the body starts breaking down. Survival requires movement. Even the bedbound require massage, or muscle weakens and skin rots.

However, Western, post-industrial humanity walks less and less, associating the need for laborious walking with class, with lack of resources, with poverty. It is hard for an audience to regard its own daily, unremarkable walking ability, minimally skill-based, as a visible sign of intellect or talent, a credible form of art making. Yet, performative walking practice is now a form of contemporary public art precisely for these reasons—because, when a vital aspect of our humanity is at the point of being lost, artists take note. And artists are walking, everywhere.

Artists are seeking to challenge our increasing urban indoor passivity, taking us outside our stasis to see, listen, think, and feel—to experience—reconnecting with each other and Nature before it is lost. Artists seek to reject viewing the world only through digital images, energy-efficient windows of climate-controlled rooms, fast hybrid vehicles, mobile phones or computer screens, giving us the gift of full perception through immersion. They seek to see, hear, smell, taste, touch, feel, think, and remember the forgotten, to experience something through our minds and bodies. To shiver in the woods, sweat in a jungle, and thirst through a desert. To see the visible and sense the invisible seeing us, fully experiencing through all our organs of perception—again.

A culture is how a specific people, in a specific place, in a specific moment, choose to portray themselves to each other and to the world. Artists are choosing to walk in order to regain control of our being from government officials, political parties, religions, corporations, and media. Artists are walking for you and me; artists are walking for us.

A Working Definition

I strive to understand what it is that I do. What is a socially engaged practice? And what is the role of performativity within my public practice? For me, the answer shifts year to year, like a migrant. Below is the definition that I am currently working with. The one constant in my ongoing reflection is that my practice remains a riverbed of rock that holds an ever-changing wild river of thought:

A socially engaged, public performance practice is
...the site-specific embodiment of urgent social issues
...through considered human gesture, such as conscious walking,
...ethically made and generously shared with a community
...as a form of diagnostic, collective, poetic portrait,
...freely offered for aesthetic appreciation and meaningful reflection,
...ultimately seeking a socially transformative, cultural experience.

Before reading on, I invite you to visit the glossary. It lists a selection of the terms I use, as I define them, which may be helpful in answering questions along the way.

Part One

Walking Practice

One Walks One

My humanity is very prosaic. It often challenges me with its child-like wants before a walk, and with its recovery needs after walking. However, when I finally walk, something transformative happens. The walker is the true me. I do not mean that "the best of me" walks. It is much more than that. It is about the coming together of all-of-me, finally achieving a healed unity during the walk.

I walk neither as a needy body, nor as a utopian thinker. I walk as one with myself. My self is finally unified by the walk. Brain and body become mind. And in becoming mind, I am mindful; I walk mindfully. And in so doing, I walk as One with Nature.

This is a Oneness that is greater than I. It is not about the fusion of two different but parallel realities, but about one ultimate reality that requires inextricable moving elements. Walking vanquishes the inner and outer duality of the human animal, and of humanity and Nature. Walking unifies the interiority of the walker, and walks it back to Nature, completing and reintegrating the walker, and thus, completing Nature.

Nature needs us. We both lost when we were separated. We, too, were an important element in its internal balance.

Flowing Stillness

In 2003, curator Saralyn Reece Hardy and I created a project at the Salina Art Center called *Becoming the Land*. I invited the grandchildren and great-grandchildren of Kansas homesteaders and farmers to revisit their ancestral landscape with me. There was no verticality but that of our bodies: flatness in every direction. It was like walking on water across a vast green ocean. My body dissolved during that prairie walk. My mind experienced no envelope. I was everywhere, and everywhere was in me.

There is invisible movement to our visible walking, another territory beyond the one ahead. We actually flow in every direction, far beyond the envelope of the permeable body. There is little edge to us.

We are dispersion. We can be smelled far away by nonhuman animals. We emanate breathed air; we emit scents; we drop discarded skin cells and hair; we produce the gassy and solid waste products of nutrition. Our evolving thoughts and feelings hover silently around us and beyond, as a kind of tentacular energy field.

When we walk, we are invisible motion in visible motion. We simply have to become aware of this invisible biological motion. We have to exteriorize that awareness. That is perfect walking practice, from the first to the last step, and beyond. If we understand and embrace this, much of the anxiety of walking practice will dissipate because we are moving perfectly long before we walk perfectly.

However, even as we are invisible flow in visible motion, we are also invisible stillness in visible motion. We can flow visibly but remain inwardly still.

Stillness is not physical inertia. Stillness can happen in the midst of brief and durational motion. That is why our performative movement can communicate stillness. Our visible and invisible flow can communicate inner peace.

Curating Walking

Walking belongs to everyone. I do not own walking. No one artist owns walking. Just because one artist has walked "successfully" does not mean that walking has been "done" and should not be funded and performed, again and again. Walking is not about the modernist myth of originality.

Walking eliminates the myth of achieving something original in the arts because everyone walks. That is why walking as art is so hard, because it dwells outside the notion of artistic talent and crafty skill. But that is the healthy system of checks and balances within the practice that keeps it humble.

Pragmatically, in terms of the success of a walking project, it is much wiser to walk an unknown path with a known gatekeeper or stakeholder who can introduce an artist to all the human and non-human inhabitants of that path, conveying the message that we can be trusted, that artists are not trespassing or invading with an intention to exploit and steal.

I cannot stress enough the importance of a walking facilitator, of someone who invites the walker to walk. This facilitator entrusts us with the mysterious responsibility of walking their landscape, translating it for us before the walk or during a first walking experience. Of course, perhaps they may strategically push us into a solitary walk of their landscape because solitude is key to understanding it. Or they may push us in with little introduction because they want to see what we experience, our capacity for seeing and whether we experience what they experience, if there is synchronicity of meaningful, sited experience. It may be a necessary test that we need to pass. However, it is fine not to pass it. Only if we experience sited meaning are we the right artist walkers to engage for their project.

I have been through many a walking test. The most challenging have been the ones I passed, but that then ushered me out because I saw more than the hosts wanted me to see and were ready to reveal. Or because I saw something that they did not consider important and kept trying to dismiss, but I considered crucial. We both agreed on the need to walk the landscape, but we saw different landscapes in need. Thus, the right walker match must happen at many levels of engagement.

An artist may be invited to walk a landscape of past human incursion like abandoned farm fields, former industrial compounds, or blighted urban neighborhoods. But even what seems ruined, abandoned, shuttered, and empty has inhabitants, known and unknown owners of its many layers. All landscapes, all visible and invisible layers, have official and unofficial gatekeepers and stakeholders, as visible or invisible as the layers themselves. All landscapes have acknowledged and unacknowledged stewards of terrain, and thus, human and non-human, static and kinetic repositories of verbal and nonverbal memories, which may be the sensitive information a walking project needs and wants to harvest—or not.

For example, non-human animals embody landscape memory through instinctive behavior, by digging, burrowing, crossing, sprinting, flying over, perching, nesting, hunting, grabbing, tearing, chewing, gnawing, pecking, calling and singing along a path, providing numerous qualities if we watch for the specific non-human animal identity of that path.

It may be that what the walker recognizes as the most important harvest is in contrast to an institutional host's notion of a proper harvest. The host may have wanted a beautiful, sunny horizontality, but the walker has uncovered a deep, shadowy verticality. Can these disparate readings of terrain be combined? It will take a lot of trust and work, but in doing so, the walk will be richer because it will offer multiple readings of the real.

Decolonizing Walking

John James Audubon walked incredible distances with his dog and gun, identifying, killing, and impaling birds to paint them. Every one of his lovely paintings is the tombstone of a bird. The history of walking is contaminated by the pale, masculine virus of colonialism: by the fever of "discovery," of being "the first man" to arrive and step into an "unknown" territory.

The colonizing notion of walking erases the native peoples in two ways. First, it erases them through the attribution of discovery as a mythical form of authorship, as if the heroic discoverers were authoring a new land. Second, the conquest, oppression, and eventual removal of the native peoples obliterates, so that those who follow in the discoverers' footsteps find paupers, social nobodies considered subhuman, confirming the white myth of discovery. Nevertheless, even if there are no visible human owners of a place (which assumes a sedentary society though some owners are nomadic), there are no uninhabited and unclaimed territories under the Earth's sky. Non-humans have ownership of territories, too, even as human, aggressive anthropocentrism has always dismissed it. Animal rights need to expand to include land ownership.

Currently, mapping technologies are increasingly producing a new generation of white walkers. Art students and young artists, a predominantly white population exposed to "new media" in art schools, are increasingly seduced by advances in hand-held mapping technologies. More and more artists are walking and mapping while walking coastlines, waterfronts, boundaries, lines, and edges.

I understand market value. But how are these new maps ecologically and socially useful to those sites, if their playful, printed rendering never transcends the notion of a drawing pinned to a white wall, for academic "interdisciplinary" review or for an art show? Interdisciplinary processes that produce traditional-medium art products, evaluated and exhibited traditionally, are bankrupt. There is no amoral gesture. There is no amoral step. All steps outside a studio are to be questioned. Those steps are either ethical or unethical. There is no making outside an ethical regard. If a site is threatened or endangered, contaminated or polluted, will a mapping artist-walker help it receive more attention that will lead to more protection? Sites have the right to make such demands.

Socially engaged practice has the right to make ethical demands of its aspiring practitioners. Those ethical demands are what makes the practice social. The practice is not just a new making methodology and form; the practice is about a resulting, socially transformative effect. Without social transformation, traditionally defined art-making in a social context is nothing but the perversity of style. The socially transformative is the difference between a static product and a living product.

I am not interested in testing new technologies and feeding the celebrity persona of a walker who turns territories into spectacular stages. The only myth that walking practice should support is the mythical qualities of place, which an artist-walker may experience to study, perform (witness), document, promote, and help protect. We need to understand once and for all that the ephemeral, mythical, public embodiment of people and place is not an entertaining spectacle but the meditated performativity of consciousness and so requires ethics.

Short Walks

In her epilogue to *The Dirty Life: On Farming, Food and Love*, Kristin Kimball's candid page-turner about her transformation from freelance writer in New York City to farmer in Essex Farm near Lake Champlain, she writes passionately about her drive to divest and move to a small place, to a village or hamlet where one can get to know everyone, where one can become known to everyone. Kimball also seeks a place where she can come to know all patterns, large and small, the reasons behind patterns, and their disruptions. I particularly love the short walks she takes with her husband Mark to watch things grow at the end of their workdays.

I admire publicly heroic stands but believe in the greater sustainability of privately heroic practices. I believe in a multitude of short walks, in unassuming daily walks for countless reasons, from the pragmatic to the poetic. I value the acquisition of the humble habit of walking for every form of getting and gathering, for thinking and feeling something through, and for getting lost so as to be found.

I think of the many walks of Jane Austen's female characters, their constitutionals, as well as the no-social-standing expression of lacking a fancy carriage or riding horse, but only having a pair of legs with which to connect with destiny.

Elizabeth walks for miles to visit her sick sister in *Pride and Prejudice*, arriving at Bingley's house with meadow-muddied skirts. Jane Eyre desperately walks miles away from Mr. Rochester to escape a haunted man's deception, a wintry walk that almost ends in death from exposure were it not for fellow women. Most of Austen and Brontë's female characters crash against the rocks of masculinity, envisioned like tides navigated through long and short walks. Their characters are built by walking alone, mostly unseen.

The long and short unseen walks of these unforgettable characters are perhaps the most powerful walks of all, because they encapsulate the human condition. They contain all the drama and depth of the epic, because the epic does not ultimately rely on scale and spectacle, but on length of endurance and depth of thought and feeling, on a psychic rather than a material landscape. And because during a short walk to a gate and back, a seemingly insignificant walk to nowhere, during an existentially fenced walk, a character achieves temporary freedom, profound insight, decision to act—irreversible growth. The harmless short walk around a garden can be a manifestation of incredible will achieving astounding goals.

Meaningful Steps

We do not need to know the destination.
We do not need to know the way.
We only need to know ourselves.

This applies to our walking. We may start with a daily walk. But the result of this novice practice is to become a walker who walks meaningfully at all times, in all directions. There is no wasted step, no step in the wrong direction. Because all meditated directions walk us to consciousness, the entirety of one's being is consulted, and thus informs and leads every step. It is a meditated mobility, fully conscious, even when not-knowing where our steps might lead.

The result of weeks, months, and years of meditation is a meditative way of being, so that we live in a state of meditation. There is no beginning or end to the meditation; it is a way of life, of meditated being.

True meditation practice should result in a meditated life. The meditated life may be initially constructed through scheduled meditations, but it is ultimately not the threading of moments of meditation with non-meditative states in-between, but of constant, meditated thought, and continuously meditated action: of living in a state of meditation.

Some think that meditation is an exercise limited to a daily or weekly set of hours, enacting it as a compartmentalized activity. They pursue a boxed meditation gesture, forcing it into a packed schedule, like fashioning and parachuting a hermetic, steel compartment into their social grid. And while that scheduling muscularity may be helpful for a busy beginner, meditation practice transcends boxing and scheduling. The point of meditation is not to fill every possible minute with appointments, racing between them.

There are no meaningless gestures. Like Nature, the economy of consciousness contains no vacuums. There are no meaningless steps. Meditation practice seeks to discern the purpose of every step we wish to take, and the effect of every step taken, seeking the meaning of it all. All steps, fast or slow, in any direction, amount to meaning.

Path Into Paths

As far back as the Greek philosophers, we have meditated on the fact that everything is constantly changing, that a walker cannot step into the same path twice. Heraclitus would have said that neither the walker nor the path are the same, both are different every time.

A walker knows that knowing a path is not merely walking it from beginning to end. A true walker knows that knowing a path requires walking that path in both directions, because things look totally different when seen from opposite directions, practically forming two distinct experiences through opposing views.

One path is really two paths, depending on our direction. In every round-trip, the end is the beginning and the beginning is the end. Thus, every path has two beginnings and two ends. And we must walk a path night and day, so that we see what dwells in the light and in the shadows. But the light, too, has a range, as the shadow has a range. We must seek to experience what dwells in the soft and in the harsh light, on the edge of the shadows and in the deep shadows. All seasons. We must try to see what dwells in the cold, in the hot, and in the in-between. We must walk that path every month for many years, so that we experience birth and growth, peak and reproduction, illness and decay, so that we see the cycles of life and death of the path. That is true path knowledge; that is true walking practice.

Do not just walk along a path. Talk with a path; dialogue with a path. Speak with your mouth, talk with your hands, and talk with your feet. Listen carefully with all of your body for its responses. See what it presents you with, what you find and what finds you. Seek to be found by what is visible and invisible to the human eye. And if you are healthy enough to walk it barefoot, feeling the soil with your soles, touching the rocks and tree bark with your hands, a truly tactile walk, learn through the nonverbal, learn through your skin, so that you experience the skin of the path.

Of all the places I have walked performatively, the nation of Hawaii is the place where I have experienced the skin of the path most vividly. During the summer of 2011, as I prepared a walking performance entitled *Speaking in Silence*, I often felt that I was walking across the rugged back of a giant turtle out to sea. The island of Oahu seemed to move beneath my feet, shaking my steps. I was constantly feeling as if I was falling. It was a dizzying sensation I could not shake off. I often had to reach for my balance, holding on to walls and large stones. It made me feel particularly vulnerable, as if the mother turtle could deep dive any time and leave me alone in a shark-infested sea, to be devoured or drown. Everything seemed to vibrate as part of an unseen ancient metabolism.

A walker knows that the point of pilgrimage is walking, that walking means shedding. Pilgrimage is about what happens along the path in terms of releasing unnecessary, visible and invisible baggage, from fat to hurt. Walking is psychic editing. The path is editing you, clawing at you. The path of pilgrimage can be an aggressive animal—of your own bloody making. A path is arduous because we have made it arduous by not being prepared for it. A path rejects unreal agendas, if not the agendas of the unreal. Because a path is pure thisness.

The Spinario Walks

The Spinario is a Greco-Roman statue showing a young male shepherd, a youthful long-distance walker sitting down on a stump, carefully removing a thorn from his left foot. I saw it during my first visit to Italy as a high school senior. It was one of my first exposures to figurative sculpture that was neither mythical nor heroic. It impressed me as modern long before modernity.

Decades later, I found a small copy while walking through an old barn filled with antiques in Millerton. The reproduction sat by the cash register. The cashier was using it as a paperweight. The Spinario is a much-copied Hellenistic bronze turned popular souvenir of 19th-century Grand Tours. So, I wondered whose great-grandmother, grandmother, or mother (or perhaps it was inherited through a patriarch's line) bought the miniature Spinario in Rome and brought it back to America, to a well-to-do merchant, doctor, or lawyer's house in upstate New York.

I wondered who held up this example of transatlantic voyage, bourgeois memorabilia through many a winter and remembered Italian summer walks? I held up the heavy little copy and discussed it with the shop's owner, who was unaware of its history. However, I put it down and walked away. The price seemed too high. Plus, I had not gone out planning to shop for classical sculpture that day. But somehow, I could not forget it.

One month later, walking through Manhattan's West Village without any particular direction, I found a second copy of the Spinario in a diminutive antique shop. It was a lesser specimen yet its price was six times that of the piece in the barn. Lesson learned, I returned to Millerton, hoping the shepherd would still be there. He was, still sitting quietly by the register.

After hundreds of years and my youth, the Spinario walked away with me. The boy with the thorn now sits on my fireplace mantel as I age, resting until the day I die, when it will be willed or sorted out through an estate sale and then walk again to another home, my walks unknown to the next walker in time.

Timeless Walks

In *Sissinghurst: An Unfinished History*, English historian Adam Nicolson, son of writer Nigel Nicolson and grandson of writers Sir Harold Nicolson and Vita Sackville-West (who inspired Virginia Woolf's *Orlando*), shares a moment of timeless insight after inheriting the stewardship of his grandparents' castle, famous gardens, and farmland. He describes walking the Weald and perceiving the uninterrupted continuity of its human and natural processes, like the falling of leaves into Hammer Brook at summer's end, acorns dropping into the stream's depths, or the timeless barking of a dog in the distance.

Nicolson writes of how the present is unintelligible without a knowledge of the past, both because there are places where the past continues undisturbed under the mask of the present, and because when there have been disruptions, the past is the missing body part of the now that needs to be perceptually reclaimed, so that the present is fully articulated. In Nature, the past is not past because everything that has ever lived and disintegrated is still among us in some new form.

I often struggle with language, with how to best articulate the fact that humanity created the notion of the past, of permanent loss. In addition, North Americans may be the first culture to pretend to live without the past, heightening the human animal's alienation from reality. But in Nature, nothing is ever lost, and thus, past, present, and future are simultaneous.

Whatever was once born, all that once peaked and procreated, or blossomed, fruited and seeded, has decayed, died, and been recycled into new life. This visible and invisible cycle is continuous. Moreover, all cycles, from the microscopic to the titanic, are equally important parts of the local and regional, peninsular and island, continental and oceanic, planetary and galactic cycles of the universe.

The cyclical nature of the planet and the universe means that we can walk this uninterrupted thread back to prior moments in the motion. We could call it "walking back in time." But language fails us because this surpasses time. The mentality and vocabulary of the irreversible, forward passage of time is an unhelpful approach that puts us back into thinking and acting in terms of a *past* past.

So, how do I accomplish timeless walking if stripped of language? Well, while words create realities, not all realities rely upon words. There are realities greater than language. So, all I can write is that the walker's body can begin to achieve this if we decide to perceive in this way, step by step. In my experience, it takes a willingness to open our perception, followed by a conscious decision to sustain that perception, articulated out loud so the brain can hear it, and the body has permission to enact it, which opens a normally invisible door to the yet-unknown, which the walker needs to walk through. It is not about medieval magic; it is about letting go of the filters of fear of civilization.

Walking & Death

I always hope the walkers in my projects are not seeking movement out of fear of death, as if trying to walk away from death. We walk towards death. But how we walk towards death makes all the difference.

As a monk, I was trained to keep death close to me. Death was neither a friend nor an enemy. I should neither fear it, nor desire it. I should simply be mindful of my humbling mortality at all times.

Every time I set out to walk a path, no matter how far and long, or close and short, I prepare as if it were going to be my last walk, as if I were not going to return from it. In fact, friends often scold me because I try to say farewell to them, but they do not want to hear it. I accept my death more than they do; I am readier for it more than they are.

Whether our friends and colleagues are receptive or not to our awareness of mortality, the walker must always leave his home in order. That is the best way to walk, with the greatest peace of mind, having left little to nothing in disarray, or pending. Of course, sometimes we walk to clear the mind and discern what's pending. However, I am speaking here about a walking practice at the service of others.

How can a walker pretend to resolve anything along the way if the walker has left an unresolved life back home? And yes, lessons learned along the way may help a walker resolve personal issues. But that cannot be the way of a walking practice, because the private places an unfair extra burden on a public path that may already be burdened with issues.

The best way to engage a path is when the walker is already healed and capable of healing others. Of course, to collectively walk a public path secretly seeking personal healing is a fact in the history of leading pilgrimages. But in order to take on the responsibility of leading a walking group that needs healing, or of entering a path that needs healing, experience tells me that the lead walker should already have walked through healing.

Otherwise, the group and the path may have to take care of the lead walker. However, that is unfair to them, because the lead walker is there to take care of them.

Of course, we are never fully healed of old and new psychic bruises and wounds. Indeed, perhaps we should never be, as the economy of pain is a safeguard against arrogance. Nevertheless, we should be healed enough so that we have the ability to put our story away.

/|\

Walking requires self-knowledge, even as walking increases our self-knowledge. Death is terrifying for some because it is the ultimate piece of self-knowledge, the crowning act of intimacy with the self. Death is the supreme test of our interior life placed in evidence.

Death cannot be faced well without self-knowledge. And walking, because of all its predictable and unpredictable challenges, is a unique tool to achieve intimacy with the self and with Nature, which holds our truest self. Walking is one of the best preparations for death, for our appointment with how we walked there.

Walking & Love

Walking faces us with many landscapes: there is the landscape outside of us, and the landscape inside of us. We enter a landscape, seen and unseen, but we also bring our landscape into it. We, too, are a landscape: the secret landscape of love, gained and lost, only known to us in remembered and repressed memory.

A true walking practice sooner or later confronts us with love. Everyone we have ever loved reappears; everyone who ever loved us re-emerges. They come out of deep memory to meet us; they step forward out of the shadows and into the light to watch us by the side of the road. Or they stand in the way. It depends on our secret history of love.

If we are perceptive walkers, we will see them, we will encounter them watching, the lovers we have left and been left by. If we come to this intimate moment, we have arrived at a deeper level in our walking; we are crossing a threshold. The possibility of being healed and healing has come to us.

When we begin to confront our history of love, all paths turn into a lovers' lane. We thought that we were entering a path to help heal a community or restore a landscape. But the walk is addressing us first as a prerequisite for healing others. We are the first landscape of love that must be restored.

This moment is not about meeting the memory of a lost lover, perhaps triggered by a smell that involuntarily led to a Proustian memory of heartbreak. The moment I refer to is about an accumulation of people loved and lost who suddenly line the road, who occupy and even block your path, irreversibly.

This is a pulsating threshold, a turning point in a walking practice. This is a path of love completely lined with once-loved individuals, where we remember everyone we have ever loved and been loved by, as a secret community of the wounded heart.

It may be a love walk lined with all the mistakes we have ever made in love simultaneously exposed. If we decide to cross this threshold, there is no question that the memories of our many failures in love may bruise our psychic body like overgrown, thorny hedges lining both sides of a narrow, English country road. Our body may walk bleeding, covered in forgotten blood, rehydrating old tears, but this bruising movement through old pain will mark a deeper healing for us as walkers who are walking for others.

To confront and to be confronted by everyone we have ever loved and been loved by can feel like dying. But we are not dying, we are walking profoundly, walking through our deep psyche as we should—as we must—if we are to become conscious walkers without baggage, turning uncomfortable, disturbing, and even repressed memories of loves lost into available, functional tools for loving others when we walk.

Love is a life imprint that is never erased. Past loves may not be manifested around us most of the time, but there is a point of no return to walking when they all reappear and are embraced, forgiven, and healed, sometimes to dissipation, or they begin to walk with us and never leave us again. They have forgiven us—if we have forgiven ourselves. As of then, the walker walks with love, in love—permanently. For to be in love with humanity is the ultimate prerequisite and result of walking.

Glass & Hockney Walk

For American composer Philip Glass, performance is the formal, public framing of what arises and flows from the activity of deep listening. Throughout his 2015 memoir, *Words Without Music*, Glass writes about the creative process of composers, but much of what he describes applies to the creative physicality of artists who walk.

According to Glass, a shift of sources makes all the difference in producing something that looks simple in its execution (as simple as walking), but achieves a cultural breakthrough. The art world may at first be unprepared for the art of walking, not recognizing walking as art. Indeed, the artist walker may also be unprepared to argue for the gesture, because it has been made before possessing all the theoretical arguments to defend its making. But the body knows. The body always responds ahead of the mind, and that is exactly how new art forms are born, relating art to non-art.

A walker must not only listen to the outside world, a walker must also listen to the inner world. It is only when these two forms of listening are synchronized, the outward with the inward, that the walker has truly become a walking organ of perception, a true listener—a part of the landscape.

There are familiar paths so ingrained that our feet can walk them "blindly" for us, liberating our mind to contemplate matters elsewhere. In addition, there are unfamiliar paths that, because they are deemed safe, can be walked in the same "blind" manner. In these instances, we assume that there is nothing left to see, or nothing remarkable to see. However, these are not ideal forms of walking because they use landscapes as conveyor belts for thinking.

There is a monastic tradition of repetitive manual labor that frees the mind for contemplation, a monotonous activity that supports certain aspects of complex thought. I can see how someone could engage walking in that way. Of course, that person would experience nothing except thoughts.

The most successful artist walk is when an artist walker merges walking as a creative act with the act of deep seeing and deep listening. Creativity and perception merge, encompassing the inside and outside, the above and below, the around, behind, ahead, and before. The artist walker is thus aware of possibility both before a step and as the artist steps, an awareness projected ahead of the volume in motion.

Glass also speaks of the importance of sourcing one's creativity outside one's discipline. If one is making art about art, everything will be predictable and only result in updated variations. However, when art is placed within the context of human society and Nature, referencing the social and ecological, not only does it draw from a different inventory to inform its content, but unexpected forms can be originated, such as walking as art.

British painter David Hockney returned to Yorkshire as he turned 70 to paint his native countryside. In *A Bigger Picture*, a wonderful one-hour documentary by Bruno Wollheim, we witness three years during the process. Returning to his homeland, Hockney speaks of how we see through memory, how the act of seeing is filtered by memory.

I agree that we often see through memory, because seeing can trigger memories that are then played simultaneously in our current seeing. Nevertheless, I also believe that we are truly capable of seeing without memory, which is to say, without perpetual self-reference, without the constant footnote and endnote of our autobiography.

Can we consciously surrender the ego and perceptually be in the present without our past? Can we achieve autobiographical freedom for a moment? Can we see like a fox sees? Better yet, can we see like a tree sees, as German state forester Peter Wohlleben describes in *The Hidden Life of Trees: What They Feel, How They Communicate*, "seeing" without having eyes?

I have seen without eyes in unforgettable, ego-less sight moments. We cultivate them by walking, by seeing through the ankle and the knee, by seeing through the wrist and the elbow. I try to walk like the fox, to see like the fox. This is no mimicking. It begins with getting into the brain and the body of the fox, and then, once inside, allowing for things other than thought to guide me, allowing for an unspoken unknown to drive me to incomprehensible action against thought and plan. I begin to walk like the fox to be fully here, without human memories, to see nothing but what's here. The fox avoids hounds and looks for food; the fox hides the food it finds. The fox is not writing its autobiography. And yet, it is completely connected to the moment without having to think about the meaning of the moment.

To walk the moment, seeing, smelling, and listening. Only that. One foot in front of the other. Only that. To inhabit the space between Hockney and the fox.

Walking & Performance

Walking as art practice is performative, even if this is unintended, because the moment a body wants or needs to walk and enters the space and flow of the public, joining the sited public, it becomes a public body, a body whose performing in society is watched by society, all the more as it seeks social agency.

I am not very concerned with justifying walking as art, even as I write and rewrite these pages about it, no more than I was concerned with justifying installation as art during the 1990s as they blurred the boundary between art and our cluttered, domestic and shopping landscapes. Art is but an aesthetic tool to generate meaningful and transformative experience. I am not interested in defending the credibility of any particular tool; I am interested in generating conscious experience, however I can. The goal, regardless of the cultural tool, is to experience increased consciousness.

Artists who walk as art perform; they become performers during the act. And when selected members of the public are trained to walk with them, and when members of an untrained public spontaneously begin to be moved and join them, then everyone is performing, everyone is watching and being watched; all become performers during the walk. And this is what I call *social choreography*, to choreograph movement in society, by society, which may lead to the movement of society. Social movements start with the public movement of one.

Walking & Socially Engaged Practice

Socially engaged art practice seeks embodiment but not necessarily materiality. Its concern is the generation of creatively critical, meaningful experiences and their enduring memories as the footprints of transformation. This can happen while experiencing without consuming or collecting.

True walking practice, enacted by vulnerable bodies willing to enter the unknown without weapons, disarmed of cynicism and only empowered by empathy, excludes cynical bodies. A vulnerable body seeks other bodies willing to become vulnerable with it, not as the surrendered raw material of public art, but as collaborators, partners, performers, volunteers, and audiences in a humble, strong practice. Socially engaged art practice is not about the author's body but about all the participants' bodies. All concerns as to whether a piece represents the state of the arts are replaced by whatever it takes to culturally reveal the state of the people.

Although the socially engaged artistic body may require periods of preparatory silence and solitude, socially engaged art practice is not the gesture of a studio-isolated body. The performativity of the practice reclaims the full repertoire of individual and collective connections, currently reduced to the notion that connective change can only be triggered through informed group consumption, or the refusal to consume.

Socially engaged art practice departs from the isolated, Platonic, creative method. It exits a rarefied art stage and its audience. It recontextualizes the artist's body across the commons, recuperating its citizenship, and reestablishing connections. It exits the cloister of theory and steps into the arena of action.

A socially engaged art practice is a performative practice. It automatically turns its artist practitioners into public performers, whether they are skilled in performance art or not.

The engaging presentation of challenging social issues as aesthetic experience requires a knowledge of behavioral psychology and creative skills. Critical theories, reformist ideas, and liberal intentions are not enough for the establishment of deep human connections, which require empathy, the debunking of widespread falsehoods, which demand persistence, and the communication of complex truths, which command patience. Social justice cannot be achieved without social healing.

The embodied delivery of social issues resulting in the slow construction of an ephemeral cultural envelope requires a psychic architecture of trusted perception. This is not about an artist hiring a theatrical director, but about an ethical artist choreographing people sensitively into and through the safe performativity of aestheticized gestures that support increased consciousness.

This is not a simple form of making. This complex collective process should not be fast-tracked. Once violated, trust may be lost for years, because this is not an advertising campaign with a reset button. In terms of creating a list of required stages for those who wish to engage in it, this is how I would lay them out:

1. A first stage of research consisting of extensive readings (a bibliography of people and place), informal and formal conversations, interviews, solitary and paired walks, focus groups, and charrettes, all of which result in a clearly written proposal.

2. A second stage of free public readings of the project proposal, and project promotion. There will be project concept presentations to possible co-funders, institutional partners, and community gatekeepers and stakeholders; as well as recruiting field advisors all along the way into an advisory board-in-place (a sited mentors' panel), to keep refining the proposed project.

3. A detail-oriented, accountable, public production third stage, negotiating access permits and safety, recruiting and training performers, docents, volunteers, and documentarians.

4. A fourth stage of enactment through a complex, durational staging, across one or more sites, sometimes simultaneously, with non-invasive documentation.

5. A fifth stage of evaluations, revisiting the experience through in-house conversations, a town hall meeting, one or more lectures, an exit report, and farewell correspondence.

6. And finally, a sixth stage consisting of revisiting the people and site years later in order to follow-up responsibly, because we became bonded by deep experience (once adopted, always adopted), which glues people together across time and distance through the tides of memory, through recurring waves of memories that generate a desire for more such experiences.

This is, by no means, a complete or definitive list. It is my list as of today. But every artist with a socially engaged practice has such a list, with their own unique variations. The point is to be aware of project stages and cover all the bases.

Every step of this process will push and pull performativity, in public and private, making it the medium of social practice. In addition, what is public, which is to say everything, should be transparent, if transparency does not expose an alternative project to sabotage. Ideally, transparency of project process, from beginning to end, publicly performed, is key to successful reception of delivery and the memory of delivery. Transparency generates responses and dialogue, becoming key to the checks and balances of a walking project, ultimately assuring its ethics.

Socially engaged art practice is delivered through the walker's body: arriving, entering, greeting, hand shaking, hugging, standing, speaking, bending, sitting, being still while listening, answering while gesturing, greeting some more, exiting, and walking on. The visiting walker's body meets and is temporarily absorbed into a sited collective body. Together as one, this new body becomes the performer of socially engaged art practice on the body of Nature. This practice is the creation of a performative body that is larger than the artist's body.

Walking as Recovering

An artist walker walks across a prairie or along a local waterfront. What is the use of that? Perhaps human intimacy with that environment is being lost, and there is a need to revisit, to recover. Perhaps the landscape was once closely known, when there was agriculture and fishing, all manner of harvesting; before our post-industrial workforce sitting inside all day at computers; when seasonal labor required being outdoors. Losing hamlet, village, and town populations to cities has increasingly disconnected us from fields and waterfronts, except when they are transformed into preserves and parks where we camp or jog.

However, perhaps fields and waterfronts are still well known but threatened, increasingly endangered in some way, and outsiders need to know what is happening; outsiders could be recruited to help, to bring in much-needed resources.

An artist walker may manifest a knowledge and way of life that is being lost, a landscape in danger of being lost. Humans have a way of becoming blind to the familiar nearby. Places and paths tend to become invisible to us over time, losing their history and meaning.

We are surrounded by meaningless monuments lacking in significance to generations several times removed from past rulers, heroes, saints and gods. The heroic is fragile, as national identities are taken for granted, change, or come under siege. Much cultural patrimony is destroyed this way.

An artist can help to reawaken the awareness of the psychic value of a site by revisiting and renewing its meaning, or by exposing how contemporary forces are trying to erase an important piece of history. During a project, the site can again become a destination, even if contested, a place to walk to and through, through the excuse of art.

Walking & Sex

Sex drives so much of human behavior that it is difficult to divorce it from walking. I do not mean that a walker might be looking for sex. I mean that the human-animal's sexual drive, particularly during youth, is the conscious and subconscious undercurrent of much of what the body does.

The desire to get up, step out, move forward, arrive, enter, and exit may contain an unconscious, undetectable sexual under-current even though the actions are not accompanied by conscious sexual desire. This undercurrent is not about finding a temporary or permanent sex partner, but about being driven by an ancient energy that is procreative; a basic energy connected to the way non-human animals are choreographed by survival instinct.

Not enough is said about the link between conscious and unconscious sexual drive and daily movement that seems to bear no sexual content. In a youth-oriented media culture where the old are vanished from sight or depicted as monstrous to behold, and in a male-dominated culture where virility is worshipped and fed Viagra when limp, not enough is said outside of the context of illness about how the diminishment of sexual drive with age correlates with loss of desire for seemingly sexually-unrelated daily movement. This experience is only known by the old and rarely spoken about in a society that silences the old.

Aging makes us increasingly static. Indeed, aging is often about fighting stasis. And yet, this is neither pathetic nor tragic. Stasis need not be a state of loss and ruin. Stasis has great value as a pensive moment that can harvest much insight, for it is a state of inactivity at the right stage, at a biologically earned stage of much deserved rest and potential for reflection.

There is a stage for life as movement and a stage for life as reflective pause; a valuable pause filled with memories of movement. Moreover, this is when the reality of sex as life's conscious and unconscious undercurrent suddenly reveals itself most clearly, when we are finally able to stop and remember the visible and invisible reasons for all our past walking.

Walking Needs

A walker walks because the body needs to walk, to step forward, because the body needs to stand, to take a stand—to respond. We walk as response, sometimes as the only possible, legal response, to the loss of humanity.

The body walks, even if the brain does not know its destination. The body is often ahead of the brain, but only if we cultivate this, if we free the body from the brain-cage of ideas, of only being able to walk forward as a result of ideas or in pursuit of ideas.

The body may intuit and even know its destination, long before the brain. The brain, so used to driving the body, may be understandably confused or alarmed, like a passenger strapped into the back seat of a moving car who sees no head above the wheel. But an intelligence is at the wheel: the wheel itself. And if the brain surrenders its constant need for information, for control, this experience might be the beginning of a better relationship with the body, and the environment.

It is challenging for the brain to tolerate motion without notion, to accept motion without known purpose. Nevertheless, it is during those moments of not-knowing, of walking for no reason, of walking without reason, that our walking is at its most pure, at its most connected.

This purity is not the purity of "art for art's sake." It is the essence of human connectivity, very close to the state of the animal—reclaimed. It is not about finding human meaning but about being found by meaning, naturally. Things will come our way. The path is real, because it is not the result of our brain's projections. The body is the teacher; the environment is the teacher. They are speaking with each other in a very old language, even if the brain does not understand that language.

Our steps are an unknown language being physically articulated, as if single steps were letters, spelling words, forming phrases, long sentences, incomplete until we reach a corner, turn left or right, pause, remain still, look, listen, see, and are found by understanding.

Walking Stillness

Silence is not the absence of sound.
Silence is the absence of distractions.

Following this thought, I believe that stillness is not the absence of movement, but the absence of disturbances. We can walk with a deep inner stillness that is not shaken by movement. We can walk with a deep inner stillness that informs movement.

Movement informed by deep, core stillness is not necessarily abstract and unproductive. Movement informed by stillness has the quality of considered gesture, regardless of pace. The gesture may be very slow, and thus, prolonged. Perhaps it is being explored, so that the gesturer is watching his own gesture unfold. Nevertheless, a considered gesture may also be manifested quickly because it has the wind behind its back, it is walking downhill, pulled by gravity—or it is like a bird, in flight.

We can embody stillness in motion.
We can manifest the movement of stillness.

Walking the Child

As an adult viewer, I was formally trained to appreciate the whole of a painting. As was my custom, I once stopped to observe a large landscape painting newly exhibited in a museum. After seeing the whole, I then considered the painting's depth of field, its near and far, the earth, sea, and sky. Next, I saw its larger details, what populated it, and if there was a human narrative. Finally, this was followed by seeking its smallest details, like filigree across a surface, thus completing the whole. But on that day, a child suddenly stopped next to me. He interrupted my vision and gave me the gift of seeing things differently.

The child immediately pointed to a minute detail within the painting, inviting me to see it with him. It was the first thing he saw! In fact, it was so miniscule that, at first, I did not see it. Actually, it took me great effort to see it. And I experienced the sudden realization that, as an adult, as much as I excelled at encompassing the whole of a landscape, I increasingly missed its microscopic perspective, the instant pincer-perspective of a child who did not start with "the stage" but sought the individual, be it farmer or field mouse.

Since that experience, the rest of my adulthood has been spent trying to recover that perceptual perspective while walking, not at the expense of my mature perception of the whole, but as the often-lost, precious child-like element that adds to the true totality of perception, and can thus perceive a landscape from either perspective, starting with a grain of sand, or a towering mountain.

Interruptions

A body may start to walk, and then interrupt its walking for hours, days, weeks, or months. That does not mean that our walking has stopped. Indeed, our body may have walked so much for years, perhaps over a lifetime, that long after it stops, it has become the body of a walker, and it continues to walk in our rest, in our sleep. We walk in the stillness of no walk. We are always walking, even when we do not visibly move.

Walkers are connected. There is always someone walking somewhere in the world. Multitudes. Walking is greater than any one body. We may think that our walking is interrupted. But once we have started walking and become walkers, there are no interruptions. Walking is a global river, always flowing. I believe that we can deep-walk consciously by compressing time, joining our walking ancestors, joining contemporary walkers, and the walkers of tomorrow. The flow is in all directions.

In Hawaii, the native people believe that their ancestors walk ahead of them, opening the way, protecting them from the known and the unknown that is to come. In other native cultures, people believe that their ancestors walk behind, protecting their backs. We walk with invisible others.

Our step creates the past.
Our step creates the future.
The present is but the length of our step.

Our thought processes are so deeply connected to walking that we walk like we think, slow or fast. Our pace can be determined by the speed of our thinking, and the speed of our thinking can be determined by our pace: we think fast, we walk fast; we walk slowly, we think slowly. We walk with determination, up or down, straight ahead or meandering, constructing or dismantling arguments, alternatives, one step at a time, thought and step as one. It may all sound very simple, but it is an intricate brain-to-leg choreography that took thousands of years to develop as our brains expanded and thought took the place of instinct.

Walking the Animal

Despite the occasional home video about dog feats posted on the Internet, with canines walking on their hind legs for longer than usual stretches, non-human animals do not walk the way we engage in walking. Non-human animals move from one point to another, seeking food and shelter, migrating and mating, but as far as we know, they do not walk for the sake of walking.

Walking for non-survival reasons is integral to the construction of the human animal. Walking allowed the human animal to begin to experience vertically, to begin to perceive above and beyond the ground. In fact, humans domesticated dogs to listen to and sniff the ground for them. Dog companions on a walk substituted ground-level perception while the human increasingly thought and thought, increasingly disconnecting from the environment. Moreover, while our alienation from Nature is tragic and needs to be undone, this separation is the basis for the civilized notion of human transcendence, of existence above and beyond Nature.

Sustainable, consistent, collective, vertical movement marks the birth of the human-animal's civilized notion of transcendence. But thankfully, in trying to undo this alienation and begin to construct a new, Nature-based notion of transcendence, the human mind is not restricted to the brain. The deep body thinks. The depths of our organ-wide, distributed mind are not brain vaults filled with forgotten or repressed elements only unleashed during dreamtime or trauma. The elements that make up the mind are everywhere in the body and interact with each other, particularly when we are not thinking, sometimes most productively during thought-free walking.

It is important for a walker's wholeness to recover the early human experience of listening to and sniffing the ground, of experiencing survival needs, and of walking without thoughts. This combination is what can make a walk whole, in terms of walking the full human animal beyond the limits of the fantasy of civilization.

Walking with Trees

It has been a decade since I last listened to the nonverbal voices of trees while walking. I wrote a passage about it in *Sited Body, Public Visions*, an intimate text about performance that I published in 2007. The act of listening to urban trees has become a memory, perhaps because most of what they communicated was deep pain, and an intimidating but understandable rage.

Therefore, I have not tried listening yet to the trees on the land where I currently live, a former pasture reclaimed by woodland, which I have been restoring for several years. Those trees are making a now-undisturbed comeback, and I can only hope that I am not making mistakes in their stewardship because there are many opposing views as to what constitutes woods management, from zero intervention to the elimination of invasives and the strict promotion of native species.

Ten years ago, there was a period when I walked slowly around New York like a forest ranger. I walked the city in silence, mindful of my breathing, cultivating no thought. During those urban walks, I would touch the trees. They were on planters along the sidewalk. Many were littered with garbage, enduring daily doses of car fluids, dog urine and excrement, not to mention the seasonal salting of city streets. Most were bruised and scarred: their trunks bore terrible lacerations from vehicles backing into them. Their lower branches were mangled by adults trying to access their cars, or torn by kids playing. Their upper branches fared no better, violently "pruned" by tall trucks. Sometimes an entire tree would be a monument to mutilation.

Most newly planted, young urban trees were reasonably content and quiet. They still wore protective netting and were framed left and right by wired stakes. But when I touched the older ones, it was like listening to wrenching groans emanating from deep in the earth. My hands did the listening. It was not a question of my ears. My hands absorbed their sounds, like vibrations, the way that the hearing-impaired perceive music. Listening to them required a silent pause, no-thought, first touching with one's fingertips, carefully; finally, landing the palm, as if laying a hand on a child's chest to feel a heartbeat. Stroking the oldest trees was like caressing crocodiles, their bark a hard, leathery surface that somehow managed to ripple imperceptibly under my fingers.

Some of the elder trees struck me as infinitely sad, while others seemed furious. I felt as if they would have blindly lashed out at me if they could. What I perceived to be their state informed my walks with pain, and ended up making me touch less, walking with my hands close to my body, like walking through an alley of beggars with no alms to give them, only my ears to hear them. It was torture. It was sometimes more than I could bear. Sometimes I would also encounter young trees who had recently been violated for the first time and stood ravaged, in shocking incomprehension of what had happened, utterly confused. I do not know who was hardest to listen to, the old or the young. Nevertheless, I am glad that I had these terrible experiences, because they taught me that mindful walking was a way to listen to everything, even to trees.

Walking the Future

Walking surprises artists with the unexpected because they are not in control of the path. The natural path is not greater than the human-animal body because the body and the path are one. The path is greater than our civilized brains; the path is greater than the brain of civilization.

Therefore, walking may reveal what civilization does not believe in. Walking may surprise us with what does not exist in our brains. In fact, walking may shock us with what our brains deny but suddenly experience as existing along Nature's path, questioning our civilized beliefs.

The so-called impossible comes to meet us along the path, and then it is up to us to decide whether we are going to continue disregarding it as part of the explanation of a complex, visible and invisible greater reality, beyond the ideations that constitute human civilization. Or we may embrace it, even if carefully and quietly, as one more piece of the mystery that is rarely seen in the expanding universe. Maybe we are finally expanding with the universe as we walk.

I have been walking, empty of thought, and fragments of past embodiments have unexpectedly flashed before me, as well as images of my next embodiment. I have been here before. I will be here again. I am walking through lives. Without causing me to stumble, I already see my next embodiment, my next childhood and youth, even as I am still here as this walker. Without stumbling, I suddenly do not see the gravel, bushes, trees, and sky, even as there is a physical world around, ahead, and above. I catch a glimpse of an unseen next path.

This walk through Nature and our passing nature, it is nothing special, as Japanese Zen masters have often written about the experience of enlightenment. It seems special if it has not yet been experienced. But, once experienced, it is simply one of many moments during a lifelong, deep walking practice, humbling moments that are no different than finding beautifully polished, perfectly round pebbles, which one considers briefly but leaves in place along the path, forming its ground.

The conscious do not hold on to the notion of consciousness. Because consciousness is not an achievement, a ribboned medal, but a way of being that eventually permeates everything we do, and is forgotten as second nature.

Walking Urban Memories

From rural to urban paths, each path manifests change in a unique way. In New York City, change is often marked by the passage of retail spaces such as restaurants, stores, and stands that appear and disappear.

During midsummer 2016, I set out to walk across Manhattan to have dinner at the Spring Street Natural Cafe, located on the corner of Prince and Lafayette streets in SOHO. It was the restaurant where I dined with the first friends I made when I moved to the city. Over the years, I often met there with colleagues to discuss projects over lunch. It was flooded with natural light, its tall wide windows framed by lush tropical plants inside and large planters with trees outside. It had one of the few affordable vegetarian menus in SOHO, and it was vast—we always got a table. I sometimes sat at its corner-most table looking at the flow of artistic humanity rushing to and from galleries.

As I walked through SOHO that midsummer evening, strolling south along Bleecker Street, through a West Village landscape changing abruptly as small shops lost their leases, announcing closing sales while their next-next door neighbors already sat dark and empty, as entire commercial blocks were overturned, I was suddenly confronted with a new, hip, cosmetics store occupying my beloved café's former space. Cosmetics had replaced nourishing.

My brain reacted with shock as my body approached the new store's bright slickness. As my brain registered the change, my body felt a strange revulsion and began to walk away from the establishment, even as my appalled brain wanted to go peek through its windows. It was one of those moments when body and brain collide, when thoughts are but passengers to muscular actions.

It took long minutes to unify brain and body again into mind; the mind that is more than the brain, the mind that is more than the body: the mind that is the unity of it all. All of me is mind. My cerebrum is mind and my toe is mind.

I still remember that moment, months after it happened, because my body continues to reject that removal and replacement, refusing to return to the area as if it was contaminated with radiation and my approach would immediately cause me to vomit.

The restaurant was probably forced to close because of an unaffordable rent increase, as was happening to the entire neighborhood, but the speed of its replacement was just as shocking. Its erasure was so complete that it felt violent to our ability to create and sustain memories: it looked as if it had never been there, as if I had merely imagined it all along. There was no residue to hold on to. And because it was not replaced by another restaurant, I could not sit inside and taste dishes from a different kitchen, giving it a chance, hopefully continuing to be nourished within a space filled with memories of friendship that made it sacred, the way a little autobiography can be filled with secret, secular, sacred benchmarks.

Recalling that lost midsummer night, I remember how my body turned around and began to walk away as fast as it could, almost running like a hunted animal. Even though it was getting late, I actually walked back across the city to another vegetarian restaurant, the Village Natural, on Greenwich Avenue in the West Village. As I approached it, I remember that my brain began to wonder how long before it, too, would be erased. Indeed, this second restaurant was practically empty. It read like an ominous sign. I sat and ate as if during a wake, suddenly hungrier than previously, not because of all the extra walking I had done, but because my body was storing nutrients, preparing for loss, in case more might be lost.

There is nothing more disturbing than the betrayal of perception, when one's familiar reality is violated because its known markers are erased. It is different from walking an unknown territory, where markers are not established yet and, in fact, our first walkthrough is about beginning to establish such markers. Of course, we can replace most markers; most of us eventually do, as life is loss. But sometimes the loss is so profound that it symbolizes the end of a chapter, of an era. The loss connects to our body and its own changes, life's changes. Perhaps we, too, are growing old, and the loss of a place signals the loss of a life in place.

New York City is like the Palace of Versailles because of its constant stream of incoming youth. It has been written that no one was allowed to become ill and die at Versailles. The Château was about youth and beauty. The deterioration and slow pace of aging bodies is a rare sight that makes the fast-paced young pause. It even makes some think briefly about their future. NYC is a hard place for experiencing old age. I have often heard the young comment that "they do not want to end up like that" after meeting a senior on the streets. Sadly, the comment feels Darwinian rather than empathic. There is a back door exit to the city, farming out aging citizens north and south. As exciting as it is to walk among beautiful, young walkers, it is a tragedy for the practice to erase the old. Old walkers contribute a grounding element to the practice, allowing young walkers to learn from studying a lifetime of motion, from witnessing aged motion.

Walking the Imagination

Imagination is a precursor to walking. In fact, imagination bookends walking practice. There's no first step without imagining the path and the journey, its travails and destinations. Even if we surrender our imagination at the portal to a path, before our first step, seeking to walk with no thought, completely open to stimuli, our imagination is what greets us after the walk, reactivated, to help us process what we experienced.

As biographer Linda Lear writes in her detailed biography *Beatrix Potter: A Life in Nature*, imagination is a precondition to taking action, from restoration to activism, allowing us to imagine the potential and the value of something that may look ruined and seem worthless. Imagination allowed Beatrix to portray the natural world for children, which led her to walk England's Lake District, first as a tourist, later as a gardener and landowner; and finally as a philanthropist who, after her death in 1943, donated 4,300 acres to the National Trust for Places of Historic Interest and Natural Beauty, the greatest gift of Lakeland at the time.

It is not the exception but the norm that a solitary adolescent who studied mushrooms in the woods and backyard wildlife (often considered vermin) walked that far, in spite of ongoing academic dismissal and artistic underestimation as the eccentric daughter of conservative Victorians, a spinster for most of her adult life (she married William Heelis at 47); against all odds, she became a successful children's book illustrator, self-taught farmer and Herdwick sheep breeder, becoming an activist for cultivated land preservation. The walker of great imagination is an agent of cultural, political, economic, social, and environmental change.

The imagination of the walker completes the experience of the road. We need a great imagination to walk through reality, for reality is so vast that only our imagination can help fill what our intellect cannot encompass.

Walking Histories & Responses

A public art walking practice often begins with a private walking practice. I encourage all to write their personal history of walking.

I remember a pre-pubescent boy with a high-pitched voice who callers mistook for a girl over the phone. He nervously walked alone to a grocery store to ask for a quart of milk from a burly salesman, who made fun of the fact that the boy had the voice of a girl. That timid boy might have never taken that humiliating walk again until his voice was stronger. But he did, again and again, in order to help his family.

I remember being that shy boy sent out by himself to buy milk. Back then, my parents had lost everything as political refugees and we were impoverished newcomers in an inner city, working-class neighborhood riddled with hungry, stray dogs covered in mange, mounds of garbage, bullies preying on the weak, homeless alcoholics, old beggars, and pickpockets. I walked alone to the corner store with shaky confidence, while my paternal grandmother anxiously watched from a distance, perched on our second-floor apartment balcony, looking to make sure that my walk was safe.

It was a terrifying walk through the cracks of society. As an adult, I have revisited the site only to discover that the journey was but half a city block. However, it was a psychologically vast space for that child. Nevertheless, grandma made it safe by watching over me from above, like a bird. And after arriving home with a quart of regular milk and the correct change, I felt great pride, as if I had walked for miles pursuing a heroic task. That first walking errand was a rite of passage, marking the beginnings of my increasingly unsupervised independence, earned through my ability to be trusted with service to the family. But it was not a conscious walk.

I began to walk more consciously because I began to be awakened by training. By then, I was an adult who had received monastic training, learning how to read, meditate, and pray while walking inside a cloister. I also pursued training in education and psychology, to understand how human animals learn and develop.

I got training in running, biking, and dance, to displace my body efficiently and gracefully without hurting it. But throughout, my evolving walking practice was not yet an art practice. I was walking as the product of belief, knowledge, and exercise. My walk had no cultural value, only personal value. It was often public, but not about and for the public. Yet, those were my necessary secondary steps.

I can assign the transformation of my walking practice into art practice to the U.S. invasion of Kuwait in 1990. Watching the nighttime bombardment live on CNN jolted my body. My body could not watch the real-time bombing of a city without responding with movement. Violent, destructive movement called for peaceful, healing movement. That witnessing moment was the beginning of a decade of conscious, creative responses through body movement: first, moving before a camera, creating performative art photography, video, and eventually, beginning to walk performatively in public, seeking to role model an awakening, undoing the physical passivity of American society.

The year 1990 marked the beginning of being asked to watch real-time acts of destruction and death on television—as spectacle. It marked the beginning of becoming increasingly dulled to violence—as entertainment—by watching human tragedies live, without needing to physically move away from them, to run, to gesturally interrupt and try to stop them. It was the beginning of a distancing process that has led to our current, profound sense of powerlessness. Because there was nothing we need do, we did not have to walk away, to escape; we did not have to walk closer, to confront. We did not have to engage in the walking and gesturing our body does when challenged by real-time harm nearby. Reality had become distant, and thus, unreal, and this new reality-television would give us sedentary bodies, leading to increasingly inert selves, disempowered.

The body has a different relationship with a mediated event, with an event that it watches after the fact, than with watching an event live knowing that people are dying at that moment. That moment causes a different psychic effect. Live violence and death fall deep into our subconscious, generating deteriorating effects across the spectrum of our perception.

Susan Sontag reflects on this in her book *Regarding the Pain of Others*, arguing that, as of that moment in media history, distance began to erode our emotional lives as witnesses of real-time tragedies, because compassion is a volatile state that must be quickly turned into action, or it becomes cynicism and sentimentality. A viewer's long-term physical inactivity engenders anger and substitution, ranging from viewer frustration that inappropriately blames the victim, to the sentimentality that chooses to watch a Facebook video of orphan puppies over watching a public television documentary on war refugees.

On the morning of September 11, 2001, I watched the first tower of the World Trade Center collapse and had to walk away as fast as I could from its toxic cloud, breaking into a run as it caught up with me, running breathlessly until I got home to close all my windows, as the cloud filled the neighborhood. Years later, I still experience a full physical stirring, from my gut to my limbs, when airplanes fly low across a completely cloudless, bright blue sky. I would not be experiencing this physically if I had watched it on TV. I crave experience because I seek reality.

I began walking as art practice as an embodied response to an undeclared American war, my performative walking becoming even more public during the invasion of Iraq when our right to question warfare was twisted into not supporting our soldiers and into betraying our heroes by politicians who cheapened heroism. We depended on a volunteer army often composed of minorities, or Midwestern, culturally isolated, poorly educated, unemployed, rural white youth. A heroic fantasy recruitment, because everyone who enlisted was automatically labeled a hero. Therefore, my body began to walk through American war memorials in perfect silence, from Charleston to Chicago.

When I think back on this journey's twists and turns, there is a figure that appears at the outset and has never been erased by distance and time, and that is my paternal grandmother. My grandmother lived a quiet life. She grew up in a tropical manor house on a palm plantation outside Havana. She was the youngest of three sisters. Angela, the oldest, considered a beauty, was a talented poet and pianist who died tragically in an insane asylum. My grandmother married and had three children, a girl and two boys, the oldest of whom died of meningitis, a loss that desolated her. During the Great Depression, her husband had a nervous breakdown and she was forced to seek office employment, but those turned out to be some of the happiest years of her life, suddenly free from domestic chores and surrounded by new working women friends, earning her own money. I was her third male grandchild. The first two had nannies, but she raised me. By then, my grandfather had died and she was deep in mourning. It seems that raising me raised her back to life.

I left for the monastery after studying art. My exit devastated her. She visited me there once, but she was already noticeably ill and died of cancer shortly afterward. Since I was a cloistered monk, I was not able to obtain permission fast enough to reach her deathbed in time. I literally walked into the hospital room where she was dying, surrounded by our family, seconds after she exhaled her last breath. She had tried to wait for me but her body could not hold. She was still flushed and warm when I touched her. She was dead, but I whispered into her ear, telling her between tears that I was there, that I had finally arrived.

My grandmother's life is being erased by time. All that remains of her are yellowing old photographs, a rosary and art deco jewelry she was able to smuggle past communist soldiers when she fled Cuba, and scraps of her handwriting. Grandma is already unknown to her family's current generation. Her maiden name was Pino Dueñas; her married name was de la Vega. Her Spanish first name was Amparo, which means shelter. A private woman who died in exile forever yearning for her motherland, of which no poems, essays, or biographies shall be written, remains at the root of my practice. Because she looked over me while I walked for the first time on my own. Because she made sure that this child was safe. And I, too, have looked over my students and performers since then, making sure they were safe.

Part Two

Roadside Spiritualities

Sustaining Sight

As a child, I walked head down looking for fragments of coral, shells, pebbles and seeds. As an adult, I sometimes walk like that child, curious about the treasures of terrain. It is wonderful to reclaim and re-experience that first perspective, that hungry sense of wonder. But as an adult, I know that it was not wonderful to have been scanning and harvesting from nature for my personal cabinet of curiosities, because I was depriving mollusks of homes and birds of food. The practice of deep walking is not about collecting.

After art school, as a young monk, I remember an early training period in which I was simultaneously engaged in editing the senses and opening the senses through voluntary poverty, manual labor, vegetarianism and fasting, monastic studies, periods and degrees of silence, chanting, meditation and contemplation.

At the peak of that cloistered period, I took a walk beyond the walls, in much need of psychic expansion. I started to walk up a thick grassy hill and, while climbing, began to look down at the vast, sloping green carpet ahead of my uphill steps. But a sudden deep sight stopped me. In that instant, I could see every individual blade of grass among thousands, among millions, each one unique yet similar, same but different.

I no longer saw Nature in a grand sweep. I finally saw its minuscule, intricate parts. I still remember that moment of expanded awareness. The instant I saw that singular blade of grass, I saw them all, fully alive, layered but as individually distinct as you and I. It was the kind of walking experience that takes over the body; it halts your body and throws back your head to face the sky in a kind of walker's ecstasy.

I do not remember how long I stood still, standing on top of that hill, physically held within deep sight. Eventually, my walk continued downhill, and I made my way back to the abbey. Outwardly, I seemed the same, but, inwardly, I was suddenly focused, more than ever before, so profoundly focused that this began to change me, to make me look for more such moments of full perception, seeking to sustain deep sight for all of life.

Walking Time

"The past and the present live alongside each other in our working lives, overlapping and intertwining, until it is sometimes hard to know where one ends and the other starts."
James Rebanks, *The Shepherd's Life*

Time is non-linear. Linearity is the illusion of human mortality. Reality is complex and mostly unknown. There is no time, or perhaps we could try to say something more comprehensible through a time-based language that cannot comprehend much outside linear time: that there are simultaneous renderings of time and timelessness.

Approaching the uncracked mystery of being, I sense that I have already walked this walk, that I have already walked all the walks I know and do not yet know in the mind of time. Thus, regarding the walk at hand, the one that is about to begin, I am simply going to try to remember it as best as I can. Remembering it constitutes my creative identity and practice.

I have already walked this walk and I am merely going to remember it accurately. In order to remember it, I will walk it as if for the first time. Indeed, remembering will give it form, for memory transforms the humble act seeking perfection.

We have a choice in the kind of memory that we are eliciting. If we choose that an experience should become a memory of transformation and joy, then, that is what it shall be.

I walk through the veils of this mystery, catching glimpses as they part. I approach this mystery along the subtle boundaries of knowledge, as it appears and disappears from my awareness. The mystery can feel sad, of course, because it communicates loss. But for now, as I remember the walk before as the walk ahead, with all who walked and will walk with me, I feel joy.

Moreover, yes, I am not unaware that maybe something else is going on. Maybe this is not about timelessness and memory at all. Maybe this is an inexact articulation of some deep and complex quality of experience I am tapping into. But it does not matter, as this is not a scientific treatise but an artist's reflections on the complexity of walking, reflecting on the subtlest layers of this creative practice, of generating socially meaningful and transformative aesthetic experiences. I am willing to live with the embarrassing inexactitude of that.

I do not know how others walk. I can only speak about how I try to walk, vulnerably, trying to explore what feels like the simultaneity of past, present, and future invisible territories through psychic acuity. It may strike some as ridiculous, as stretching beyond believable grassroots scholarship. But this is an embarrassing practice, the lineage of the village's witchy idiot, the town's prophetic fool, and the city's mad visionary. All those categories speak of a child-like, creative, critical outsider walking dreamland. Indeed, they are inexact elements found by the roadside. Nevertheless, they are experiential elements of subtle perceptions, as important to understanding the complexity of the human condition as seeking the exactitude of science.

I am not a scientist, a daring theoretical physicist like cosmologist Stephen Hawking. But he imagines that if we could travel to what is popularly known as the beginning of the universe, as we approached the infinitely dense singularity before the Big Bang, approximately 15 billion years ago, time would give way to space to the degree that there would only be space and no time.

So I will argue that for artists who walk, the more they integrate into place through no-thought, the more they integrate into space through no-mind, the more they will approach a miniscule time-framed experience with a titanic psychic effect for their life practice: a sense of timelessness, followed by a sense that there is no time, an insight open to interpretation, from poetic metaphor to sidewalk activism. In the end, what we call the spiritual may be our primitive name for glimpsing a science we do not yet know.

Walking Myth

In *The Lure of the Local*, art critic Lucy Lippard writes of how public art practices have the potential to raise awareness about unknown and little known stories and memories, furthering the evolution of consciousness. For Lippard, artists can make stories and memories more public, revealing the human ideologies and experiences that have shaped a place. Such practitioners can model evolved creative responses that can support human rights, and help restore and preserve webs of natural cycles manipulated by human ambition, by functional and dysfunctional human interventions in need of review.

This process is not about artists as readers who choose to manifest their reading. This process is about artists as humble, entrusted students of place, as grounded scholars who walk the landscape as a library, giving up their personal reading preferences, allowing themselves to be led to unknown readings, ultimately pointing creatively to the many contradictory texts a place often contains. Artist walkers are entrusted with a diversity of rooted texts in local code. An artist's job is not so much that of an editor, but of generously voicing a public that is often without voice, crafting a careful reading by everyone for everyone out loud.

Like Lippard, I advocate the performative invocation of the mythical as an effective tool for the public manifestation of people and place through pre-scientific ideologies, helping contemporary audiences to experience the desire for transcendence that past generations sought. This revisiting of old myths and new myth-making is not about the cult of the artist, about mythifying the artist or the artwork, but about helping audiences inhabit the space of myth as a valuable vantage point. Inhabiting myth can offer a transformative point of view that can unleash unknown psychic potential among participants.

Manifesting and inhabiting the mythical in a public, durational group performance always challenges our abilities much more than experiencing the mundane. Mythical experience requires us to go an extra psychic mile; it sometimes requires the extraordinary, which may feel like mere exertion in the moment, teetering on the edge of collapse, but is always remembered as greater than itself.

Memory has a way of transforming the challenging pursuit of the manifestation of the mythical in a performance into an enormous individual and collective achievement, remembered as a new and amazing myth.

Bodhisattva Walks

The Judeo-Christian tradition has prophetic walkers like Moses, John the Baptist, and his cousin, Jesus of Nazareth, but little is said of their walking. Historical and mythical attention concentrates on the agency of their stand, in terms of commanding, baptizing, and preaching to the masses at chosen sites: Mount Sinai, the River Jordan, and the Hills of Galilee. However, they walked to get there, they made followers walk there.

Christianity had a tradition of wanderers known as *gyrovague* monks who spent their lives walking, often in pilgrimage, and were received as guests by *cenobite* monks, who lived in a cloister with a vow of stability, of rootedness to place. But the first chapter of the 6th-century *Rule of Saint Benedict*, which eventually reformed all monasteries and convents in Western Christendom, gave the gyrovagues bad name as walkers unable to settle down, always on the move following their independent will. In a medieval world where individual and collective will was surrendered to heavenly and earthly autocratic rulers, the notion of bodies whose movement could not be contained and surveilled was threatening to religious and secular authorities.

In addition, during times of plague, an unknown walker was suspected of carrying disease, prevented from entering a village, and even chased away. During the Inquisition, a free-spirited walker could be accused of witchcraft. During famine and poverty, an unfamiliar walker could be suspected of poaching, burglary, and kidnapping children. During war, a foreign walker could be accused of spying, torture, rape, and murder. Perhaps it was not until the Romantic period, coinciding with landscapes increasingly free of predators and bandits, that walkers began to be perceived as idealists seeking inspired destinies. In 21st-century America, if walking happens outside the realm of athletic display and Nature appreciation, from hiking and climbing, to bird watching and counting, a walking artist can be suspected of a tricky laziness, of a purposeless activity lacking in quantifiable productivity.

For me, perhaps the most attractive of the walker myths is the Buddhist notion of the Bodhisattva, of the enlightened body whose heightened awareness is manifested through the public gesture of walking individuals and groups toward increasing consciousness. Nevertheless, rather than enjoying life among the newly conscious, the Bodhisattva leaves them and walks on to facilitate the journey to consciousness for others, in other places, forever starting it anew. In this construction of a walker, the state of enlightenment is a state of pilgrimage, of constantly walking with new people.

Cloister Walks

It is easier to attain material detachment and some degree of consciousness when one commits to a cloistered life with a flexible rule of silence that edits superfluous talk, a vow of celibacy supported by a celibate community's friendships, voluntary aestheticized poverty, and a life behind protective garden walls, than trying to achieve these states in the world. Having experienced both lifestyles, conscious life in the world is harder than life in a monastery, for all its sensual privations.

It is interesting that monasteries provide for walks as tools for the attainment of consciousness. There is the humorous notion that monks are not supposed to run unless there is a Viking invasion, of which there have been many, some deciding not to speed-up but to be martyred for stillness. Monks are encouraged to walk slowly throughout the monastic enclosure, designated for meditative walking. But even work areas are considered to be meditative space, in terms of the Benedictine notion of *ora et labora*, of pray and work, of praying as monks engage in manual labor, which only employs the body and frees the brain for prayer.

Cloister walks follow the square and rectangular paths of monastery courtyards, their walls often lined with the 14 images of the Way of the Cross, a devotional practice which requires the walker to pause, meditate, and pray before each station. The images show another walk, the painful, uphill walk of Jesus carrying a cross, and all the people he met along the way. This is a sheltered walk that meditates about a daring walk synonymous with taking on and carrying the so-called sins of others. It follows a notion of walking as cleansing, which requires the sight to see the burdens people carry invisibly during their walk. It constructs a collective healing walk through the sacrifice of the leading walker's body. Indeed, the leading walker's suffering body evokes an empathy that is, de facto, the cleansing agent for collective healing. Empathy for the one taking on the burdens of others opens the sight of the public, turning them into witnesses, which is a deeper state of viewership, inviting them to reconsider their past, present, and future movement.

Cloister walks are not about distances incrementally achieved. A body walking a square, rounding its corners, walking the four sides of a square is a body going nowhere. But what if we measured this psychically rather than materially? What if we measured the miles in terms of psychic distance to an invisible destination? Because materially, there is nowhere to go but within.

In spite of appearances, the cloister walk is not a horizontal walk. On the surface, the architecture is visible: a walled garden. However, the true architecture lies below the surface: the vertical architecture of a bottomless well, or a topless mountain. The "farness" of a cloister walk consists of psychic verticality. The walker has no destination in the known world. The walker approaches the mythical. The walker combines the underworld and heavenly elements of Orpheus and Dante with the mission to walk the caves of his subconscious and the mountain paths of awareness toward full consciousness.

This second psychic architecture only opens up through the repetitive walking of the same space: day after day, week after week, month after month, year after year; decade after decade. You might say that the repetitive walk of the same path, in fact, is what creates the ultimate architecture of self-knowledge through the surrender of visible achievement, creating a walk that confronts all illusions of achievement, and vanishes them from the path.

A cloister walk is also about reading. The monk often reads inspired writing, biblical commentary, theology, hagiography, and mystical treatises during the cloistered walk. Deep reading while walking a cloister alters pace, slowing steps, sometimes marking moments of insight with the cessation of step, before resuming reading, walking on. In robes. To walk wearing long, flowing fabric vanishes the legs but emphasizes each step the way a ship's entire body sways right and left in heavy seas. Fabric swings to and fro, like a pendulum. In this rhythm, a right is a clear right, and a left is an indisputable left. To suddenly stop in the middle of this creates a material disruption only fixed by the downward pull of gravity.

The cloister walk is a highly choreographed private walk in the shade surrounded by protective walls, with a pool of bright light in the middle, where there is a birdbath, a sundial, a cross, a statue, or a plant specimen blooming or fruiting seasonally as a reminder of creation's cycles. I invite performative walkers to consider a silent retreat in a monastery to experience this form; considered step, sustained slowness, and punctuating stillness as an ancient training which is not provided in contemporary art schooling.

Walker Blueprints

A walker's experiences and perceptions form the subtle blueprint of a conscious life, drafting a true walking practice.

My blueprint can be summed up as made from inherited, experiential, and chosen elements, like an existential equation that has temporarily inhabited the planet: lose everything as a child and grow up as an immigrant, in poverty but with dignity, surrounded by sad but wise old women who remember the past vividly and pass it on to you as a form of wisdom. Study religion, history, literature, psychology, and ecology, seeking to understand the small and great forces that produced your world; choose installation and performance art as a subtle visual language of welcoming metaphors; spend silent time meditating about the world from deep within a monastery. Spend time doing urban social work among the homeless and people with HIV and AIDS; live in a populous city, a diverse cultural capital, cohabiting with fellow immigrants from all over the world as an experiment in democracy, but more importantly, in Oneness. Travel the world using art as an excuse for activating memory and experiencing some degree of healing; and begin to discover that Nature is not the background to the play of the human condition, but that there is no separation. Finally, conclude that we need to deconstruct the mistakes that have defined civilization and reintegrate into Nature. Consciously seek to begin to perform and sustain performative actions from this holistic insight in society, no matter the abundance or lack of resources.

These are not instructions, but a description of what I see drawn across my blueprint. In it, conscious reintegration began by mindful walking and inviting others to walk mindfully with me.

Destinations

Walking a road becomes so important for some that it overshadows both their arrival at a destination and the destination itself as an extraordinary site, no matter its history, scale, and sacredness. The transformative experience of the walk makes the destination post-climactic. The true climax happened during the journey, while walking the road: one or more breakdowns followed by release and surrender, one or more insights leading to transformation, long before arrival. Yet, had there been no destination to journey toward, there would have been no process for transformation. Even when a destination becomes post-climactic, it was necessary because it triggered walking; it made us walk.

Walking can be about desiring and achieving a form of psychic death, in Western monastic terms, the death of the man or woman of the world, so that they can become empty vessels and the universe can finally begin to trickle or rush in, filling and overflowing them with the right contents for others to drink from. Sometimes, after such a journey, we remain forever journeying; journeying becomes our interior life and our public practice.

Nevertheless, when group journeys are sterilized from the messiness of the human condition, as folks travel within air-conditioned, padded bubbles, riding on powerful wheels, walking very little in-between places, destinations become important because they are the main source, and sometimes the only source, for potentially transformative experience upon arrival. Other than being herded like sheep between entry and exit, there is little or no walking experience after having been transported and deposited there. The transformative thus relies on the fact of briefly being there. Others accomplished the pilgrimage for us, which poses the question: "was there was a pilgrimage at all?".

Regardless of how we get there, our presence at a destination regarded as mystical landscape or historic architecture means bearing witness to the identifiable embodiment of an ancient truth that may be potentially imprinted on us, like an inerasable tattoo. Of course, there are folks who wake up with a tattoo after a long night out and do not remember how it happened, because the space of pilgrimage became a mere in-between. Not only was pilgrimage curtailed, but they were not there to be present, but to consume a sight.

If people are truly present at a site of pilgrimage, it may provide them with a psychic blueprint that produces existential scaffolding in reverse, like skin that finds a skeleton. The destination stands as their material reminder of who they are supposed to be, to keep becoming, and to forever remain. They experience a reengineering marker that can rebuild them as a human cathedral, chapel, church, mosque, shrine, stupa, synagogue, temple, or zendo. In fact, they may never need to pilgrimage again because the destination is now forever within.

Magical Walking

As an adjective, the term magical is defined as a moment or place that seems mysteriously removed from everyday existence and exerts an effect, from delight to puzzlement.

Magical thinking is not escapist childish fantasy. The magical is the language of Nature, filled with the complex webbing of myriad visible and invisible cyclical patterns, including the patterning of chaos, of chaotic patterns with a purpose. Chaos serves a violent flushing and recycling purpose in Nature; the problem is that humans often stand in the way, by accident or folly.

If animals could voice in human language, their descriptions of what is would be communicated through what would sound like magical speech, not because animals are non-scientific, but because they accept and inhabit our planet without doubts or apologies, as living elements of a still-expanding complex universe.

As a walker, I seek to enter this complex web so that I can walk in all directions and dimensions, even if I only seem to be walking along the pattern that we humans see. I have no words with which to accurately describe this walk, really. All verbal efforts are incomplete and embarrassing.

If magical language is the medium of fools, then foolishness is a requirement for walking.

Multiple Paths

The body transforms natural environments through human passage. However, because the discourse of walking is anthropomorphic, I am always seeking non-human perspectives. Therefore, I need to acknowledge that there is no such thing in Nature as territory without paths.

Nature is already crisscrossed by visible and invisible, infinite paths. Myriad paths preexist human steps everywhere. Everything is path: big or small; up, down, and sideways; through the through. There is no space that is not the path to some form of life. Large bodies are paths to small bodies, and they to the microscopic.

Life is a path to life. The path of the louse and the tick across skin. The paths of earthworms, ants, and termites. The slithering path of the snake. The path of the hedgehog, possum, and raccoon. The paths of the fox, coyote, and wolf. The path of the moose, the deer, and the bear. The air paths of birds, migrating. All have paths for foraging, scavenging, hunting, and storing away. The elephant's path to a place of death. The path to the bones. High above dry ground, low to the ground, and underground, in shallow and deep waters; most are tragically being destroyed directly and indirectly by the illusion of human path making.

Human paths are only valuable as metaphors for reading the real. Paths are only valuable if they lead us to reality. All paths lead to the reality of our Oneness with each other and all there was and is.

I am the walker on the path, the dirt on the path, the air on the path, the sky above the path, the soil beneath the path, what grows along the path, what flies over the path, what swims by the path, what lies behind and waits ahead. I am the other walker I meet on the path. I am I and not I.

There is a path, there is no path; there is a walker, there is no walker. If illusions are the condition and the language of humanity, let us use illusions to create conscious paths; let us perform the illusion of beautiful, wise walks that point at the reality of consciousness.

Psychic Topography

We are complex energy forms not fully contained by moist mineral bodies. We are permeable fields of energy with undulating edges and tentacular wisps. We experience by moving and by being moved. Human stance has moving roots, uprooted as flow, and re-rooted as healthy pause. I have often dug in the area where a tree died of disease or age, felled by storm or chainsaw. Long after a tree is visibly gone above ground, I still find large fragments of powerful roots underground, like decaying, thick limbs without a body, a lingering substantial presence that whispers subtly about a former body in an ecology. Underground parts can outlive an above ground whole, leaving a buried presence that should never be underestimated.

Human experience can leave sited energetic residue as part of a former life attachment to place. The effects of intense experience can overflow from a body and leave an intangible rooted imprint, like an invisible footprint in the shadows. Different cultures regard this suspect or believable mystery as the witnessing of ancestors, spirits, ghosts, visions, apparitions, hallucinations, hauntings, or poltergeists. Terms depend on secular systems of disbelief, or pre-scientific systems of belief, and the negative or positive charge of the experienced post-human residue. Original narratives may eventually be lost altogether, passed remarkably intact, or grotesquely embellished over time, making the footprint amusing or fearsome.

Some walkers are like Geiger counters, whether aware or unaware of their perceptual skills, of their ability to perceive such residue in various degrees. Unfortunately for our walking, secular institutions and programs do not train us in developing psychic acuity, a term explored by Lewis Hyde in his book, *Trickster Makes this World*. What I still wonder as a grassroots scholar is whether these contemporary field experiences, walking through the residue of extraordinarily painful past human experiences invisibly and indefinitely locked into place, are activated by anniversaries of pain or by post-human territorialities, the way those in pain become defined by pain and defend it, rejecting healing, having lost all perspective and hope, dwelling in personal hells revealed to walkers as the psychic topographies of place.

Walking triggers many questions about past human-animal conditions. Do these footprints also enjoy a lingering mind, and thus, a fuller post-human life than we perceive? I do not know. Some walkers experience the misfortune of being in the path of a tiger, or a ghost. Tiger and ghost were neither hunting nor haunting. They were merely enacting themselves. The walker finds and is found. The point is to gather diverse information that leads to empathic understanding, which concludes in knowledge that matures into wisdom about whatever is visibly and invisibly experienced along the path.

As a walker, I believe that these psychic markers are an important part of the experience of walking. They must not be dismissed; they must be embraced. They are a critical piece of the recorded and unrecorded, official and unofficial, historical record while experiencing a walk through a site. If we believe in the stored muscle memories of a body, we should be open to considering that these extraordinary moments are the stored memories of the body of a landscape.

Sadhu Walkers

The sadhus of India, the wandering naked ascetics, were believed to spend their entire lives crisscrossing the country. However, in Sondra Hausner's insightful ethnographic study, *Wandering with Sadhus*, she writes that many sadhus stop wandering at some point in mid-to-late life, settling down to practice in place. Life becomes about sited practice, teaching through anecdotes, communicating wisdom extracted from their memories of walking.

At that point, it is my belief that a psychic wandering begins; that the road now lies within the former walker: past destinations are now inside the older walker, who remains walking, even if currently seated and surrounded by disciples, wisely transmitting the walking. The older walker walks the memories of a lifetime, remembers his forward walking in time, and walks on, to nonmaterial destinations, as the possibility of nirvana, or yet another incarnation approaches to keep expanding consciousness.

The earned stillness of an older walker does not erase his muscle memories, the effects of a lifetime of walking. One is a walker forever, moving or not, because one has achieved detachment from everything, even from walking, because walking was never the end in itself.

Walking practice engages in detachment for the sake of achieving an expanding sight, the sight of our Oneness. We walk to physically and psychologically step away from attachments to people, possessions, and places, seeking to achieve freedom from self, desire, and baggage. Walking is about detachment from the parts to see the whole, even as the whole is expressed in the parts.

We are embodied. Everything, even what is disembodied, is expressed through the body. Even the immaterial is expressed through the material. The immaterial uses the illusion of the material to talk about what matters. Steps talk. Mindful walking through the material world is one of the building blocks for consciousness of the immaterial.

Buddhist Walkers

I believe that deep within the well of Buddhism is a foundational doubt about the existence of God, a core doubt that threatens the illusions of theistic religions. Buddhism shrugs this off as an honest theistic hesitation that makes Buddhists not spend too much scholarliness on building a theology, but rather, on creating the ethics for a healthy relationship with what constitutes reality, seeking our increasing awareness of reality and realistic compassion as opposed to sentimentality.

Buddhism spends its scholarliness reflecting about the illusory human persona, trying to diminish its ego-based impact on the planet: the body in Nature, the body of Nature, the body and Nature as ephemeral. This reminds the human animal that its identity and its surroundings are temporary, while developing a conscious stewardship of the body and its resources.

Buddhist teachings invite us to walk an unknown path with no promise of safety, but with thoughtful suggestions: walk carefully without hurting what you find along a path. Do not kill lions but avoid being eaten by lions, though your death and the death of the lion are inevitable. Next time, you may be recycled into a lion, and the lion may be recycled into a human. Your roles may be reversed when you find each other again. Then, perhaps you may understand his hunger, and he may understand your fear.

I like the metaphor of meeting the lion, because Nature is teeming with biting and stinging, poisonous and predatory life. Nature may try to eat you alive. Shark attack survivors testify to this. The true walker knows this and does not need to feel safe under the protection of a heavenly patriarch. To be one with Nature, fully reintegrated, is the walker's true protection, the attuned state of the holy animal who is defined by perception: who knows the way, who intuits the way, who finds the way, who gets out of the way, who avoids the wrong way.

The Buddhist walker is aware that he kills too, that every human step crushes plants and insects. The walker apologizes to them with each step, and in between steps. The Buddhist walker's steps begin with a silent desire for forgiveness as the foot inevitably rises, a silent request for forgiveness as the foot humbly thrusts, and a silent plea for forgiveness as the foot sadly falls, each time. This invisible trinity of desiring forgiveness takes a lifetime to achieve, but once ingrained, it is the invisible mechanism of the Buddhist walker's step, walking the mantra of forgiveness.

We take turns being each other.
We have been all others.
There is no Other.
We are One.

Walker Stages

In *The Graveyard Book*, Neil Gaiman tells the story of Nobody Owens, a lost, cold, and hungry, orphaned child who stumbles into a historic cemetery where the ancient dead take pity on him, so he is adopted and raised by the ghosts of the graveyard. Only, Nobody Owens does not know they are dead. He hears them talking and sees them walking; perceiving them is his normalcy of sight. In fact, he sees the dead and hides from the living, because the living are the truly scary.

In her "Diary: In Fukushima," published in the *London Review of Books*, Rebecca Solnit mentions how one of the major problems that Japan tsunami survivors reported was the presence of restless ghosts of people washed out to sea, who lingered seeking direction and needing appeasement. The survivors lit large bonfires along the beaches for the ghosts to see and walk to, so they could find their way home.

As a walker, I seek to see everyone and everything, no matter how embarrassing the tale of nobodies nowhere I may end up telling, after my walk.

Try to envision going to sleep one night and deciding that, when you wake up the next morning, you will be in the same bed, in the same room; but it will not be the same. Nothing will have changed and everything will have changed, because you seek a change of perspective. The walls will be there, but you will see through them. The room will be full of things visible, and previously invisible; what you saw and what you did not see before.

Until this moment, what you saw was what others wanted you to see. But from this moment, you are free to see beyond. This is what a walker may experience, a perceptual revolution. You need to give yourself permission to see all there is, visible and invisible. You need to give the universe permission to show you all there is, visible and invisible, because the universe will rarely force this on you.

You will become aware that you are here and everywhere at the same time. You are alone and with everyone at the same time. At first, this may all feel like a huge revelation, like Buddha's moment of enlightenment under the Bodhi tree. But as Zen Masters say, enlightenment is no big thing. Enlightenment happens, and then it becomes second nature. It has always been this way, and it will always be this way. You do not become a saint when you experience enlightenment. You just see more.

As a walker, harvesting this new awareness, aware of all paths in all directions, you are finally ready to walk in any direction. You are. And wherever the flow takes you, you are going to see and listen to everyone and everything. You have embodied the comprehensive methodology of full perception. And this begins with a decision: the decision of wanting to see it—and walk it.

$$\overline{/|\backslash}$$

A successful walking practice is not the result of a mathematical equation. But there are subtle stages to undergo when it becomes a lifelong practice that amounts to a way of living, becoming the walker's identity.

When we start walking, there is a first stage when we soon realize that we live in a world of signs, that the road is full of signs. We find signs, and we are found by signs. Indeed, we may be or wish to become a sign to those watching us walk everywhere and nowhere.

In the novice walking stage, we often seek to comprehend the meaning of all signs and symbols, forcing wisdom. But all forced wisdom is faulty, because it is premature. We may try to connect two or more signs or symbols, seeking greater meaning. There is a lot of effort to a novice stage, like being a magician's apprentice. And while there is gain from sincere effort, in the end, it is just a matter of time. Walking practice needs time.

Nowhere is often the territory of the forgotten, suppressed, repressed, denied, or hidden; the dominion of the scary, terrifying, embarrassing, guilt-ridden, or shameful. All that is missing is to complete the story of a people and a place stored in the vault we call nowhere.

Everyone carries a secret notion of the place we call nowhere, of what must not exist in order for our worldview to continue to make sense. But we need to shed our secret notion of the nowhere in order to walk into all the unknown, unfamiliar, distant, and remote places that hold human experience.

Sometimes we must pursue a hidden truth. The ethics of our walk may depend on it. But sometimes we should not pursue what we envision somewhere, because we may become incapable of seeing what hides in the nowhere.

Sometimes we should surrender knowing, because a secret content knows exactly where to find us. The chase is in reverse. The point is to walk, to keep walking. The ultimate find is the walk itself: to have found walking.

We should always trust that finding and not finding are both right. We may just be found if we do not find. Not finding may be the prerequisite to being found. And whatever ultimately finds us along the way may be what some cultures call an unknown destiny.

If we commit to walking practice over time, there is a second stage in which the meaning of signs and symbols is revealed to us without looking and deciphering, without intellectual muscle. Suddenly, we read them clearly. Our capacity for nonverbal language has imperceptibly awakened. We quietly begin to dwell with roadside signs and symbols; we experience and understand them easily, not willing to live in any other way than within the meaningful, surrounded by the appearance of clear psychic signage and decoded mythical symbol, because that is how the true path of our life, of all life, of the entire universe flows consciously.

Walking & Worship

Humanity seeks more than food and shelter. Humanity seeks to transcend mortality. This human search shape-shifts through the centuries and decades, from worshipping mountains and trees and sacrificing to pantheons of gods or faith in one god, to believing in science and the cult of technology. Humanity worships temporary solutions to the unknown.

Walking is not a religion, but for some it can be a form of worship within their religion, a kinetic religious practice, as walking meditation is for Buddhists. But walking can also be a form of worship beyond religion, beyond theologizing, for a secular mind for which life is about life. That is the mystery of life: the meaning of life consists in that life is about life, and walking can be its metaphor. Walking can be the purest act of worship in the cult of life.

Walking Empathy

Walking, as an immersive process, can evoke empathy. This empathy results from experiencing and thus understanding the conditions endured by others, whether human or non-human.

Walking is punctuated with immersive experiences that can help walkers understand the violation of an environment that communicates its distress when the walker repeatedly witnesses the exploitation of its resources and contamination of water, land and air, the illness and death of plants and trees, fish, birds and quadrupeds. Walking confronts us with human architecture and inhabitants, whose way of life may be threatened, under siege, and with people who share their stories, actively seeking our empathy.

There is a morality implicit in walking, which starts with deciding not to stay inside, to step out into the world, to see and listen firsthand, placing ourselves within the reality of others. In so doing, we walk beyond the self in order to connect deeply with other selves, and truly get to know and feel what they are undergoing. Selflessness is the first moral principle connected to walking, at the very foundation of walking.

The selfless desire to see, to smell, taste, touch, and listen is followed by empathy. The firsthand experience of cause and effect, of struggling and suffering, helps us to better differentiate between good and bad conduct in a place, between right and wrong actions in the world, through whatever set of principles we carry as an active system of values we call morality. But because this morality is based on selflessness and is informed by experiences that trigger empathy, it is potentially not self-righteous but compassionate, forgiving, and generous, because it has experienced complexity.

Of course, there is no question that some can walk many paths unaffected, only seeing what they wish to see through the harsh filter of rigid agendas, their so-called morality untouched by diverse experience, remaining blind to the experience of others. However, I prefer the permeable, evolving morality brought about by empathy for the most unexpected peoples and places.

Walking the Sacred

If I were to create a god, I would postulate that the material and immaterial components that make up the universe are the body of god. However, even that feels limited and incomplete. So I surrender to a maxim in Christian theology which says that in the mind of the created (those who live and die) the uncreated remains incomprehensible. If there is a god, it is culturally unimaginable.

God remains the great distance. We exist in the shadow and in the light of the possibility of an incomprehensible entity. Therefore, I surrender to the fact that, for now, walking with the unknowability of the divine—if there is such an isness without beginning and end, without boundaries, here and everywhere, stretching in every direction for it is every direction—is a more accurate and humbling way of walking. Walking witnesses the one or more gods according to the culture of the path and the place, from making Nature into god, to importing god from across an ocean. As a walker, I acknowledge sited versions of god as an expression of local, regional, and national culture over time. These versions range from the mythical to the scientific, no more and no less, as culture is to be respected.

I do believe that the earth was perfect before humans exploited it industrially, consuming wastefully, not minding contamination of soil and water. There was a time when everything and everyone was in balance. It was not Eden; it was not utopia because there were predators and prey. I call that former perfect natural balance "the sacred." The sacred is a secular term I apply to an ancient object or space that embodies or contains that former balance, which should be approached with reverence for the memory it evokes and the importance of its survival for our future.

I seek to walk the sacred. I seek to reinsert myself into that former balance. But for that, the walker must be sacred, too. The walking entity must engage in the sacred. What does this mean? It means that the balance starts inside the balanced walker. My internal balance is what will connect to the external balance. These balances are but reflections of each other. We should not walk out of balance. We should not depend on a walk, on a people and a landscape, to balance us. I must first do the work of balancing myself, achieving inner balance, long before I walk.

Walking is not pretense. Walking is not theater. Walking is an expression of a state of balance we lost and seek to regain. But it must first be regained inside the body of the walker. The walker's inner universe must be in balance.

Walking Vessel

Vulnerablity is the wisest material with which to coat a strong vessel. A walker should be a conscious vessel. The conscious vessel is transformed through its holding nature. The conscious vessel receives from holding. Its cracks are mended. The sediment of a lifetime of content, holding story after story, begins to fill the cracks of its fragility, and slowly covers the entire vessel with an unbreakable patina of wisdom.

Walking engages in gathering through the psychic enormity of step. Whether only taking one, or a thousand and one steps, the courage of taking a step is transformative of the walker and of the landscape. Taking a step unleashes a visible and invisible landscape of healing content.

A step gathers as if the foot were a hand.
Whether barefoot or shod, the foot absorbs and stores the land.
It knows the land long before the brain knows through thought.
The foot stores an ancient form of wise no-thought.

Crossing Walks

I remember a mundane moment in my pubescence, when I was suddenly confronted with pale pictures and tense dialogue from a reality that I had not lived and should not have understood, but knew as belonging to my future adult self. It was presented to me through a seemingly harmless but subversive black and white television set sitting on a corner table in my grandmother's living room. I was only allowed to watch it for a few supervised hours after school, and only after I had completed my written homework, which I faked most of the time because I was bullied at school and school was torture. What I saw in silence, like an old soul unwillingly reborn and now an old child witnessing a devastating vision, was a cold distant reality that drew me in and taught me, even back then, that there was no time, that I had already lived something like that and would live something like that again, even as it was still far away in this new lifetime. The images were as magnetic as they were quietly terrifying, because I might lose myself when I got there. I might die when I caught up with it. Even worse, I might lose my soul's progress, the very configuration of a growing identity formed one life at a time; I might have to start all over again, at some lower level, in some even more unknown and unwelcome existence.

That is what I thought and felt back then. That televised reality promised but did not yet deliver a life that I might live, that I would certainly live—later—in a place not yet visited, with people not yet known, and with sadness, with a bottomless sadness. It would be fulfilling in some way but it would not be happy. I already knew and grieved that. For now, the confrontation was the onset of secretly feeling foreign, marking a point of contrast with everyone and everything that surrounded me, which was supposed to be my place of birth and my family, but which was disturbingly unfamiliar. The unknown felt more familiar and was somehow known. The images and dialogue spoke of a secret destiny that I must not tell anyone about. That moment burdened me with a secret, about myself, about desire, about a possible future, at a time when my body was still so small that it was barely able to hold the information of a new life, much less a secret so vast. That prescient knowledge made my steps incredibly heavy but I had to get there. I had to find my way to get there as soon as I could. But much of it had to do with merely growing up, with being older and somehow empowered with enough resources. I was already desperate to get there. Yet it was not about achievement and award. It was not about ownership or any particular career. All that I saw, for now, and it was enough, was a washed out northern reality, in a bitter but dry, snowless winter. There was a small white boat anchored on a dock. There were lonely drifters. There was a tall man, Scandinavian, under a dark cap, wearing a black sweater and jacket. He was upset. I was upset. Our nonexistent relationship pulled and scared me. Nevertheless, I wanted to run across the years to him and simply sit by him in peace, watching him work.

The years went by. I grew, I fled; I crossed the seas. I walked. Walking became the metaphor for everything because of the constant motion of life, to life, out of life, between lives, back to life. A lifetime went by and I did not meet the tall white man heavily dressed in black. I experienced winter but I did not find that wintry landscape or boat. Yet now, decades later, dwelling in an invisible desert, I suddenly read that the actor who played the sailor in those images has died. I had almost forgotten him. His memory was buried and might only have resurfaced at the moment of my death. But it all came back to me. He was a very young George Kennedy. It was probably an episode of *The Asphalt Jungle*, as noir as mainstream American television could get in 1961. Before the Internet, television was our window to the world. Yes, it all came back to me, like a glacier I felt it enter my bedroom, crushing everything in its path: the walls and furniture, my ribs and heart. Life was mostly done, yet I had not found the relationship and the place. I felt profoundly sad, as if an original destiny had been stolen from me by a thousand disturbances and interruptions, roadblocks redirecting me away from the ocean. I had no wisdom but I had pain. My only relationship to this loss was pain. But I was supposed to walk on and complete this meandering path, as best I could, holding onto a sense of purpose and awareness that I call consciousness; holding onto the latest form of self, a self that will be put through a pinhole and lose most of its trappings, hoping to survive with the purest awareness of that self to walk again, with love. The slippery, roadside spiritualities of the complex construct that is the human animal are a dense, sticky, staining paste, made up of equal parts basic instinct and poetic transcendence, but I prefer them to the buildings of religion.

Walking Religion

The prejudices of modernity can result in project failure, particularly when art world secularism confronts religious and spiritual material as part of the visual and gestural source-language of a project.

I am fascinated by elaborate religious processions and long spiritual pilgrimages. People often ask me if I engage in walking as a form of worship. The answer is no. Walking is not my religion, nor is it my spirituality. I think that both terms are sadly misunderstood and dangerously dismissed by the Western, post-industrialized art world as we face the challenges of a global cultural environment.

I believe that spirituality is a secular term appropriated and misused within a religious environment. I define spirituality as all that concerns the human animal's desire to survive decay, pain, death, and loss. Spirituality is all that concerns the human animal's spirit of survival.

In my experience, the survival drive of the human animal, which is popularly known as "the human spirit," generates religion but is not religion per se. For me, religion is the institutionalization and ritualization of pre-scientific myths. As such, religion strikes me as a creative space that generates many cultural products at the service of the ritualized worship of institutionalized myth.

The history of spirituality and of religion, as manifestations of our desire for survival and as the cultural products of worship, when studied objectively by artists, are vital human-condition information that should inform all art training, all social practice and public performativity. Otherwise, our training will be limited by the prejudices of secular modernity; our work in society will be missing vital information, risk insensitivity, if not the total inability to listen to the local and regional, possibly ending in failure.

Part Three

Teaching Walking

No-Thought Walking

I am not interest in creating rigid rules for walking practice. My field experiences have generated some written reflections, hoping to inform young artist walkers, to help the contemporary, interdisciplinary art medium of walking acquire one or more recognizable, performative, formal elements, if not full form. I am interested in exploring all that walking activity can generate as a practice, regardless of field, even as I emphasize cultural production. I believe that walking can be a transformative experiential component to creating ephemeral public art.

There are many kinds of walks and goals to walking. A conscious walk starts with clarity of intent, even if the intent is to get lost, so as to give up control. More and more individuals need to give up control in order to reclaim their balance.

There is a difference between the educated surrender to an unknown but nurturing path, and being self-destructive. Contemporary life can be a tightly controlled and surveilled, ambitiously fast, overwhelmingly multisensory, chaotic experience. For some, just walking down an unfamiliar but safe path without a professional goal may be the beginning of reclaiming balance.

No matter how carefully planned, a walk ultimately curates itself, which is to say that a walk always surprises us with unintended results and no results; or with nothing new, the latter being just as important as newness because the maturity of a practice is based on repetition.

Disciplined repetition can consist of the same exact gesture reperformed during a lifetime. Moreover, while there are variations, because of resources or lack of resources, the seasons, age, sickness and health, solitude or company, sometimes the best of them are the subtlest.

A conscious walker may understandably seek to have no-thought while walking. If that is the intent, the walker must be clear that to withhold thought while walking can later be betrayed by entertaining thoughts about it. Clarity here consists in having no thoughts about having practiced no-thought.

Let me explain.

The withholding of thoughts while walking requires a post-walk period of no-thought, so as not to violate the experience, which is to say, so as neither to consume the landscape, the self, nor the act after the fact. It is only after this no-thought period that the walker can begin to reflect, having allowed the no-thought experience to be as consciously and unconsciously long as possible.

We need to tame our desire to consume, including our desire to consume consciousness.

We should not rush to analyze. After walking practicing no-thought, there should be rest with no thoughts. We should come out of the experience gradually. Only later should we allow the brain to slowly return to analytical activity.

There is an expression about walking "with an open mind." However, most of the time it means that we walk with a busy brain that is constantly thinking about everything we perceive, even if accepting it all. Yet I find that constant analysis, even if benign, is a rationalized form of defensiveness, a very subtle form of still being on guard. Nonstop analysis can be subconsciously performed to mask distrust. The true "open mind" is achieved by practicing no-thought, by quieting the brain and letting the body perceive more, wordlessly.

I can walk practicing no-thought. I do not monitor my breathing any more because that is thought; that is doing something in addition to walking. Controlling one's breathing inevitably generates thoughts (even if for seconds) of one's failure or success at it. Of course, if conscious breathing eventually becomes a practice integrated into one's conscious walking, so that walking and breathing are one, then that places the walker back in no-thought.

Walking School

Teaching is like walking because it is based on repetition. Teaching is based on the repetition of information and knowledge, until learned—until lived. Lessons, tested and enriched by experience, can generate insight and, over time, wisdom.

The act of repetition is not only for the benefit of the student, but also for the benefit of the teacher. Most things are not taught well the first time we teach them. Most things are not learned the first time we hear them.

Teaching takes patient, repeated articulation, in various ways. The teacher learns that the same material must be presented in different ways over time, until the listener's curiosity is engaged by one of the modes of presentation. One mode of presentation alone seldom achieves success with a diverse audience.

The strategy of repeating variations of some material over time creates a union between the teacher and the material, not so much through memorizing but through identification. The teacher and the material become one; the material becomes the teacher's identity.

In this increasing state of oneness with the material, sometimes all walls disappear. Suddenly, teaching has transcended all classes and classrooms, and the teacher is always teaching, not in a pedantic way, but as the living presence of that material in the world. The material has become a way of seeing and being.

Walking teaches us how to walk. The act teaches itself if we are mindful, if we study our steps and learn from them. We also learn how to walk by teaching others how to walk, by studying and learning from their steps. In this process, a walker becomes the walk. In the process, a mindful group of walkers is formed. As a result, a walk becomes a school for walking for all.

Decoding Failure

The concept of failure is much worshipped in art schools as important and even vital to the creative process, as a drastic form of final editing. But real failure, the social consequences of failure, as an artist affects people's lives rather than merely wastes and discards materials—this needs to be understood in a public context.

When it comes to drawing, painting, printmaking, photography, sculpture, and installation, which is to say, when it comes to traditional mediums and raw materials, the notion of failure is a metaphor for pushing mediums and their materials to the edge of their possibilities. This may sometimes result in material failure inside a studio, which is acceptable in terms of exploring a creative process inside a safe box. Nevertheless, this is meant to be a perfecting process, not a self-indulgent process, because failure produces tons of waste dumped on Nature, by way of garbage and ensuing contamination.

When it comes to art as social practice, or socially engaged art, failure ceases to be contained within an art school classroom, an artist's studio, or a city dump. We are no longer dealing with raw materials inside a box, but with human lives and the future of communities. So, failure is not an option. To fail people is unacceptable. This statement shocks many in the art world, who feel entitled to failure, but failure is not an acceptable option when we work with sentient beings.

Of course, ignorant and innocent mistakes are acceptable as long as they are accompanied by a profusion of humble private and public apologies. However, the failure of an entire project to which life stories have been entrusted and on which the sustainable development of a community may depend, is not acceptable. The project may not succeed fully, but it cannot afford to fail completely.

The notion of not being able to afford complete failure is shocking to those used to working with ample resources, but not being able to fail is a well-known notion to the world's poor. The habit of traditional studio practice faces socially engaged practice with class issues. The poor only get one chance. This is where art-world liberalism, usually much more privileged and entitled than it realizes, is truly tested because the artist cannot continue to assume that there are no boundaries to creative field play.

The unacceptability of project failure is where theoretical art studio practice ultimately meets socially engaged art practice; it is where it encounters the experience of the mass of the world.

Detaching from Art

I believe that we need to detach from art, yet hold on to what art was about throughout most of the history of humanity: the desire to reach a state of existence that is more than mere survival, surpassing material survival by providing insight into the possibilities of the human condition, connecting us with each other and with the planet. In that sense, what we used to call art allowed for the creative expression of the mystery of the self-awareness of matter, which sought to transcend the gathering of food and water, the making of clothing and shelter, our reproduction, and our submission to religious and secular powers.

The artist walker has to become an unapologetic body. Rather than arguing on and on that walking can be art, defending walking as art, I prefer to free myself from the shackles of that tired old dynamic, of having to argue whether something is art or not. I simply state that the question, too, is dated; indeed, it is as dated as the term.

Most of the time, unwillingness or inability to consider walking as art are the result of a conservative notion of art held by outdated critics, or by a mainstream public that was lost by the art world when abstraction arrived. This is a public that holds on to a notion of art as figurative painting or sculpture; it must be educated. Walking as art also requires this same public to stop passively consuming art and start actively experiencing art (participation). But we can only participate in what we have been educated to understand as potentially valuable experience.

Walking as art requires the public to let art into their bodies because of the proximity of walking as a common experience. So, there is a loss of distance from art that is at first disconcerting, but that eventually generates an immersion in the art, because the body and life of the public is the art, transforming art into culture, or recognizing pedestrian culture (common life) as art, as John Dewey once did.

We must detach from art, because art was only meant to be a cultural bridge, it was never the destination. The goal of art was to achieve greater consciousness. And while we used to believe, through the primitiveness of patriotism, that consciousness was held by oaths to one or other form of government, or by the blind belief in one or other true religion, illustrated and promoted through art, we now believe that consciousness is held by something much greater, by something that transcends institutions and historical-to-contemporary mediums: by Nature. Human consciousness is based in Nature, even as our notion of Nature continues to evolve.

Walking can be art, and walking can be walking, just walking. But, in both cases, Nature is the path and consciousness is the destination. And there is no hierarchy to the author and the medium: humanity walks.

Perhaps it is time to transcend art in our efforts to reach consciousness and replace the old term and the old question with new terms and new questions: Are our private and public gestures, whether recorded or unrecorded, for sale or for free, evolved creative gestures seeking to create a culture of consciousness?

The Post-Art Age

We are experiencing the dawn of a post-art period; we are entering a post-art path, walking into a culture without art. Much of art-making lost its relevance to society during the 20th century. Most of what we call fine art is becoming costly high craft. However, the more generous category of cultural production, in terms of creating meaningful issue-driven, aesthetic experiences, is slowly gaining ground in the 21st century.

For most of human history, art was the label given to the formal materialization of the creative imagination as it documented life and illustrated myth and authority, communicating, promoting, and helping to sustain powerful ideologies. Art was the visual currency of a pre-digital humanity, which depended on rendering the human experience by talented and skillful hands on wall, panel, or cloth with animal hair and pigments. Indeed, art became bogged down in a contested hierarchy of materials and tools, and in the preoccupation with upholding old and new mediums which, until recently, became self-referential in content, as art pretended to hold on to a recognizable identity, anxiously making art that looked like art, often for the sake of commerce.

However, art no longer embodies the visual currency of contemporary daily life any more than stained glass or embroidery does. We forget not only that mediums have their moments, but that all languages, including the language of art, can die when fewer and fewer can read them.

I am not interested in building a new practice by tearing down another one. Humanity will always engage in image and object-making. These talents, skills, and drives seem to be part of the human condition, as the way some individuals process experiences into material for themselves and others. But walking reveals the datedness of traditional mediums as cultural language and points us in the right direction for creative making in the 21st century. Creative making finds its steps and path again, art aiming to make a culture that nourishes greater consciousness, recruiting current social media skills and strategies, inviting the passive post-modern body into action.

For me, the practice of creative walking, when performed within the more generous definition and context of culture, reclaims the original intention of all art-making, and its future. In a world cluttered with objects old and new, as I listen to a new generation speak of being post-object, a notion based on replaceability rather than on the immaterial, we do not need more things; we need more awareness of things.

Liberating Artists

I believe that walking as art practice, in terms of socially engaged art, radically changes the nature of art-making, not so much vanishing the author as liberating authors by relocating them in three important ways.

First, there is the question of inside versus outside, of moving from making art inside a studio, to making it outside: a transplant that can potentially transform art into culture by engaging audiences.

Artists make art but people make culture when they publicly claim artworks as their own.

Second, it signals the increasing freedom of artists that began with conceptual art. Socially engaged art is a peak in the history of conceptualism, so to speak, by freeing artists from the anxiety of having to materially make art in all places at all times. Artists become the moving containers of art-making knowledge, to be activated or not, if and when art can contribute to issues affecting society.

The liberation and relocation of artists is democratizing, because it places artists back into the commons through their common and uncommon skills. Much like a village apothecary, baker, blacksmith, butcher, cobbler, or midwife, the visiting or resident artist is in possession of a certain set of life-enhancing skills. If art-making were re-understood as labor, as a trade rather than a career, it would democratize the practice.

Artists have valuable, creative skills to offer in the form of aesthetic, meaningful experiences. Artists are no longer mythically conceived as dramatic entities driven to make secretly, but as accessible, creative tradesmen. Artists can be called in, like carpenters, to repair the old or build the new, in front of everyone: a public process that generates accountability from demythologized artists as accessible makers.

Third, as the acquaintance between artists and audiences deepens through available, everyday, participatory, aesthetic, meaningful experiences, the need to make and experience art begins to shift from the artist to the community. The community begins to desire making and to witness making, both as a meaningful experience and a meaningful product. The community wishes to make meaning, to maintain something meaningful, with the help of the artist, and long after the artist is gone, because it is valuable to them, and it belongs to them.

Deconstructing Stepping

We can deconstruct the act of stepping forward, the action of articulating the right hip joint, moving the right thigh, articulating the right knee, lifting and swinging forward the right leg, the right foot thrust forward, articulating the right ankle as the foot comes down, to steady it. This is followed by the torso, arms dangling or gesturing, sometimes, abdomen or chest forward. Then, at last, the neck and the head, which may sway back, unless the head pointed the way for the upper body, emphasizing the curvature of the torso, from neck to waist. The head can be like the prow of a ship. (But if the head—the nose—keeps pointing the way and the torso does not straighten up after a step, we are walking bent.) Finally, the left half of the body repeats the same gesture, like an identical twin, completing the step, hips and shoulders aligned again, feet parallel.

Some equate stepping with falling, with the constant act of falling partially, but stopping oneself from falling fully; every step a partial fall or the possibility of a true fall. Deconstructing the mechanism of stepping and experimenting with the concept of falling are interesting to choreographers and dancers, who make use of them all the time.

During a 2007 set of solo performances called *The Water Cycle*, created for the Institute of Contemporary Art, as I walked barefoot along a Boston harbor island beach in early August across sand and stones that felt like red coals, the excruciating pain made me hyper-aware of the stepping ground, each step requiring a superhuman will, having to pay microscopic attention to the subtleties of the burning terrain, to the square foot ahead, seeking to place my burnt raw foot on clumps of dry algae or dead grass, seeking mere degrees of coolness from blistering ground, seeking what was hot but not scalding.

It was like the Roman martyrdom of Saint Lawrence, the only moment in my performance history where the term endurance crossed my thoughts. I limped painfully, like one whose feet are open wounds, each foot hurting more with each step, wanting to fly more than walk, to lift and levitate above the walk, forcing myself to complete the pilgrimage of the performance in agony. Toward the end, when I thought that I would have to stop the walk or collapse, I remember finally finding a spot of shade, a jagged little patch, the dark gravel on it warm but bearable. I remember standing there like a burning bush, feeling biblical, waiting for a US Navy ferry to take me back to the harbor. I had fulfilled the artistic laws of the performative universe I had created, a set of gestural laws that did not take into account an unforeseen heat spell that New England summer.

It was remarkable that I did not stumble and fall or become dehydrated in front of everyone. (Many were following—but with shoes.) My body was unexpectedly subjected to the taxing combination of unseasonably hot weather along an exposed coastal path that was also littered with sharp stones. I felt as if I was being barbecued but held the form no matter what. I held on to the necessity to sustain, through a disciplined will, the visually formal in order to achieve transformative aesthetic experience for those following, seeking not to stick to the act but to manifest true pilgrimage, which incorporates and ultimately relies on being curated by the unforeseen. That is the best way of making theory, as written by the meeting of the formal, the natural, and the psychic.

Listening to Walking

I once found myself helping to paint a room in a historic farmhouse. I worked alongside an old master house painter. She painted like a church mouse, while I painted like a groundhog. It was embarrassing. I asked her whether I was painting the walls right. The master kept painting and, without looking at me, responded that no, I was not.

I gasped and immediately stopped painting. Wet brush in hand, I asked her what was I doing wrong. Still without looking at me, still painting quietly and without condescension, the master replied that I was making the wrong sounds while painting. Startled, I asked her to say more. And the master replied: "Listen to how I paint."

As of that moment, the master continued painting while I tried to listen—to nothing. She painted without a sound. Her wet brush caressed the wall like silk. There was no dragging, no pushing pigment into the wall. Her act of painting was so smooth it was soundless and looked effortless. I tried in vain to paint like the master, but somehow my brushwork was the noisiest gesture on the planet.

Of course, it had taken the master a lifetime to discover the fine brush that best fitted her small hand, the exact amount of paint for that brush to hold, and the slow-motion flick of the wrist that resulted in repetitive perfect brushstrokes that were part of a larger pattern of methodically covering the walls and fanning the paint out without spattering. She patiently explained that a good painter makes her first vertical stroke downward, along the sides of a wall, and then follows it with a set of horizontal strokes, pulling the paint out, toward the middle. The master's exactitude was remarkable. She never used any painters' blue masking tape. She could paint a perfect line uninterruptedly along a long border.

The master could tell if someone was not painting correctly without looking, just by listening to the sound of his or her brush. In the end, even though she gave me three of her finest brushes and a sharp scraper for glass as parting gifts, I was thankful not to have to make my living as a house painter. I am definitely too rugged a painter for the smooth walls of a fine estate. In my non-defense, I should explain that I learned to paint by painting old masonry, broken brick, and ancient stone walls, pushing thick paint into dirty crevices. Therefore, what constitutes success in a dark basement may be a disaster in a sunny sitting room.

Remembering the humbling lesson of the master house painter, I can tell how someone is walking by listening to their walk, because balance between silence and sound is a revealing and important component of a perceptive walking practice.

The sound of a walk is produced by a combination of a walker's healthy breathing (inhales and exhales); a walker's focused footsteps, silent or sonorous, depending on the uphill or downhill, and the presence of loose matter; a walker's fit body, cutting through steady breeze or wind across a distance; the inner friction of a walker's movements, as naked or covered extremities rub against each other and the body, as textiles are stretched and compressed; the response of surroundings to the walker, as creatures react by crawling, running, jumping, flying, and swimming away, or staying put in frozen camouflage, or remaining calm in spite of the approach; and the volume, tone, and persistence of a walker's voice, or meditative silence.

As teachers, we need to listen to young walkers for what their silences and sounds reveal of their evolving practices.

Message Carriers

I would like to experience a contemporary cultural landscape in which artist walkers attain the same solid, social credibility that humble, dependable message carriers once used to enjoy in hamlets, villages, towns, and cities worldwide. Those were deep cultural footprints. Walkers of day-to-day and epic narratives remain functional, performative archetypes for artists who walk.

As a child, I remember how we eagerly awaited mail carriers. We looked for their uniformed silhouettes in the pedestrian distance. We listened for their gentle steps, for the swinging of old picket gates that stuck, the sound of squeaky hinges from rusty roadside mailboxes, opened and shut. We observed their technical gestures; we learned their delivery rituals. As the child of political refugees fleeing Soviet-style communism, I lived in a poor inner city neighborhood in a small, concrete apartment compound of only six units, so we would stand watch from its balconies.

Upon sighting a carrier in the distance, up high, just entering our long street, pushing his mail bags on wheels, like a little figurine in a toy train entering a miniature village, some of us would race down the stairs and stand by the building's dark, wide portal to watch his daily performance: going over hundreds of small keys strung through a huge metal ring; finding, inserting, and turning the right little key into our common box; bending to retrieve thick packets of mail from his oily, brown leather pouch; unbinding the envelopes' tight groupings, freeing them from thick rubber bands that he would save to use again; reading our parents' names and inserting mail with the speed of light into narrow slots; and finally, the loud closure of the metallic door with a bang. I can still hear it decades later; some sounds reverberate over centuries.

Mail carriers humbly conveyed our public news and intimate secrets, raw and poetic, regionally and globally. We knew their repetitive routes, house by house, so that we could predict their arrival to the minute. And if there was a stand-in for our man, if our carrier was ill and temporarily replaced by some unknown body, we immediately noticed the numerous disruptions to the well-known performance, creating a disquieting incertitude that would be talked about extensively at the family's evening meal.

We wanted and needed the messages the carriers conveyed. Depending on the season, we offered them cold water or hot drinks. We complained if the envelopes were soiled or wet, barely readable. (Our grandmothers were experts at drying moist messages.) We chatted and paid undistracted attention to them. We were the authors of fixed texts, impossible to delete without performativity: the dramatic gesture of a letter crumpled into a ball, thrown to the floor or through the air into a waste can, hit or miss. There was sculptural beauty to a paper basket full of torn pages, like bird and butterfly wings without bodies. Or were they moths? There was a material gravitas to greetings, narratives, tourism, birth and death notices, and bills. We waited for material. Writing was sensual. Communication required the physical: a forest, trees, a saw, animals, a river, a mill, pulp, a wagon, a store, clerks, a customer, reams, a table, pencils, pen and ink; sitting, inserting and sealing, addressing and stamping, a post office, and then, walking there to send off. It may sound primitive, but it employed more than thoughts; it employed the body and made it walk.

Path Integrity

I always encourage people to try to experience walking alone, in pairs, and as groups—in silence. Therefore, when creating a new group of silent walkers, I must make a judgment call on the abilities and receptiveness of potential participants. I train walkers as best as I can. I write and freely distribute a unique training manual for every new site and group. And I take chances with borderline walkers. I embrace the embarrassing practice of taking a chance.

Nevertheless, a group walk can be spoiled by a distracted walker or by a walker with a secret agenda, whose unfocused or disruptive behavior gradually begins to sabotage the movement, concentration, and experience of the rest. A walking group experience should not become about the containment of a dysfunctional walker.

I am entrusted with holding a space, in terms of creating a safe walking experience for all. It is not only a question of personal safety, which is paramount, but of form and depth. A walker making unexpected interventions that violate our contract of trust can create an unpredictable environment that ceases to be safe for most, that begins to destroy the choreography and the depth of the experience, turning it into a veneer of experience. Even if the rest of the walkers continue to do what they were trained to do, the walk can devolve to a superficial level because no one trusts that fellow walker, so everyone is on guard, protecting their vulnerability.

Sadly, if a situation nears that point, even though the disruptive walker was trained—which included reading my project proposal (a text I share with all participants), and watching others walking for a while—yet none of that penetrated that person's armor, nothing disarmed that individual, then, I normally remove that walker from my walk. I do not enable that narcissistic or troubled ego. I send the ego home. Because I am entrusted not just with protecting the integrity of the other walkers' experience, but with protecting the integrity of art and the integrity of a path, of a psychic and material landscape.

There are voices outside of ourselves, waiting to be heard, waiting for us down the path. All paths deserve to be walked without the theatrics of ego. Otherwise, we will be deaf to those voices. A path has rights. A path has the right to demand human respect.

A walker is a gatekeeper: of the gate to the bodies of walkers; of the gate to the heart of an ecology; of the gate to the heart of a village or town. Perhaps a non-adaptive walker should not join a walking group event down a vulnerable path. It is my responsibility not to let a human-made or natural landscape become the stage for destructive dynamics. A walk is an effort at seeing, listening, and pointing to what that landscape and its human and non-human communities need.

There is no question that a walk can be healing for a bruised or broken walker if the person is humble. Many people walk humbly hoping for healing. However, healing requires trust, disarmament, and generosity. Part of healing has to do with discovering that your bruise and wound are a gift to the walk.

The healing of an individual should never happen at the expense of a group or a path, at the expense of being forced to abandon the effort of healing a community and a place. If one or more individuals seek healing from a walk and a path, that must be made part of the whole, openly or discreetly, confidentially, so that we all contribute to it, directly and indirectly, but willingly, rather than it being an act of stealing from the whole and the experience.

Silent Group Walks

To lead a silent walk is of social service because it creates the conditions for mindful perception, which is the foundation for a more grounded construction of human reality.

It is countercultural to engage in a methodology of silence. This methodology consists of defining the various kinds of silence, freely training walkers in the sustained practice of silence, and facilitating silent public spaces for audiences. The creative process leading to the embodiment of silence engenders suspicion, and its final manifestation unleashes distrust, and even anger. My performers and I have been angrily shouted at by drivers and pedestrians during our durational, silent walking performances. And we have responded with peaceful silence, letting the hate pass through us. Our silence has not been condescending; our silence has been empathic, because we understand the effects of what we are unleashing. Silence in public spaces often provides a stage for all that is raw and repressed.

It is precisely because of this individual and collective cathartic potential that I value the experience of group walking in silence, even if there is disbelief at the outset. Participants in a silent walk may mistakenly think that the instruction to be silent is a form of group control, even a state of punishment. But if the walkers can suspend their prejudices and their judgments, and trust the silence, surrendering to the experience of silence, giving up the current, social media custom of constantly commenting about everything, and the habit of talking when nervous, they will eventually appreciate silence as a gift, a tool, and a strategy during the walk.

Walking in silence brings the gift of psychic rest, of resting from the job of voicing the ego. Silence is the key that opens the door to meditation, which leads to mindfulness. Silence is a strategy that both protects the walker, like armor, and creates an open space for the stories of others to enter and be listened to in silence.

Nevertheless, silence is hard to achieve, even when walkers are willing. The Cartesian misunderstanding remains pervasive: "I think, therefore, I am." Thus, a walker may fear that deep silence will annihilate the self, drowning in silence, ceasing to exist in silence. But this fear has to do with a notion of silence as punishment (silencing a voice), engendering a mistrust of silence. This fear may also have to do with a sign of our times: obsessive overthinking. This reaction may come from a fragile psychic scaffolding constantly in need of manifesting individual identity for the sake of individual (and group) psychic survival in a cacophonous world of hidden agendas. But the irony is that what survives may be an illusion, a cluster of false selves produced by that very manipulated cacophony.

We are much more in need of psychic rest than we realize. Therefore, a walk should be a safe space where this embattled dynamic can be temporarily left at the portal to the path. Indeed, if the walk's silence is deep, the walker may be unwilling to reenter that neurotic battle after the walk. The walker may wish to remain in a healing silence long after the walk, in a silent zone in which a truer self may be reclaimed and strengthened with insights from the walk.

I believe there are both short- and long-term gains from having been temporarily unburdened from the job of projecting our socially constructed self at all times. An identity in constant state of siege, whether real or imaginary, is at risk of becoming "hard of hearing" because it is never vulnerable, because it is always on guard and, thus, increasingly dense. Walkers thank me for the silence I invited them to inhabit, even if what they experienced within was the silent storm of a scared, busy brain reluctant to slow down and be silent. That disturbing reluctance to be silent constitutes very important information for achieving consciousness.

Walkers seeking silence need to rein in the potentially destructive dynamic of spontaneous, sporadic, superficial chat along the way. Methodologically, I help new walkers achieve silence through the basic notion of achieving aestheticized walking form. By laying out a walk that engages not in a leisurely silence, but in the disciplined practice of silence as a conduit to aesthetic walking form (because silence gives us a body, a minimal menu of gestures and an observant posture), the walkers begin to engage in silence for technical reasons that ultimately lead them to inhabit silence not only materially, but also psychologically. What starts as movement technique ends as state of being.

Of course, during a sustained process that starts with an open call but then begins to lay out a landscape of disciplined, deep practice, many leave and only some stay. But I rarely have to ask anyone to leave. The rigor of the process, clearly explained since the beginning, creates a self-selection dynamic because it is not about having fun, about authoring entertainment. It is about the hard work of creating art, and making sure that art becomes culture.

Silence is like water. You do not have to be an Olympic swimmer to dive into it. All it takes is entering the shallows and wading. And as you walk deeper into the element, deep silence will do whatever it needs to do for you. Because the effects of silence are different for each one of us. It has to do with where we are in life, with what we need to hear, in silence.

Every walking group is different. No matter the walk I have choreographed on paper, based on extensive scholarly research and field experience, plus feedback from trusted advisors, I must be willing to change it as my group begins to form, as specific bodies with unique lives begin to constitute my walkers. Until then, I was dealing with the cultural notion of people. But now, I stand before its de facto embodiment. Can I see and listen to their verbal and nonverbal wants and needs? The art walk that I planned may be culturally right for the archetypal notion of an American, German, or Japanese people. But is it right for these twelve young and old, short and tall, thin and stocky individuals in front of me?

There is a lot to negotiate before one engages in group walking. Just because a number of excited individuals self-selected to commit to a poetic project, engage in training, and bravely walk for hours with me does not mean that they truly know what they got into. The reality of the long walk may not hit them until the walk begins and they are walking for one hour. Suddenly, the prospect of walking for another eleven hours falls on them like a brick wall. This always happens to someone or everyone in a group.

I have choreographed enough walks to know the stages of a durational group walk. No matter how much a group prepares, it is never fully prepared. So, do I disregard these clueless walkers? The answer is: no. I embrace good, clueless walkers, which usually can be a majority. I simply work very hard at giving them all the material and psychic tools they will need to confront that moment of terrifying realization, so as to keep walking as they were trained. And if they do, and most do, they come out on the other side in awe, after a transformative walking experience.

A Culture of Negativity

One sometimes encounters a culture of negativity that attempts to filter and ultimately spoil everything. Sometimes it stems from an angry loss of innocence that cultivates an aggressive cynicism. The rejection and dismissal ultimately creates a self-complacent, armored cultural environment that does not want to listen.

When a sincere walker is considered suspect and discredited by cynical critics, the walk is either ignored or reviewed as bogus. All hope is lost before there is a chance to walk with hope. These critics may think that they are weeding out the weaker, sentimental artists, but what they are actually doing is further disconnecting and isolating the art world from society, making art more socially irrelevant than ever.

A culture of negativity is not a culture of courageous, embodied research, but a closed culture that lacks curiosity, that has stopped growing. Historically, we used to regard this as cultural decadence. Dying empires are notorious for their cynicism. Negativity is a patch on the leakage of power, because the negative look powerful.

The cultures of former empires mistake cultural self-referencing for credible cultural growth, hailing the rehashing of well-known cultural tropes that marked their former dominance as valid, masking their secret terror at facing an unfamiliar future without power. They exercise the remnants of past cultural authority, as arbiters and gatekeepers of taste, dismissing the unknown as their angry dying act of cultural censorship.

Walking practice is intrinsically sincere, because the path edits even the most insincere. The path takes care of itself. A true walking practice walks away from negativity. Every step is a gesture of hope. Daring steps dispel hopelessness.

There is no way to sustain a walking practice but by harboring hope. However, hope requires sincerity, because sincerity is the true fuel of sustainability, assuring that the practice endures not out of stubbornness but out of conviction.

As we walk, we hope to harvest information that leads to knowledge, processed as wisdom. We hope to be free, exercising our right to walk, demanding more rights. We hope for safety, and walk away from violence toward refuge and rehoming.

The peripatetic scholar, the non-violent activist, and the refugee walk. Sincere thoughts and feelings, sincere goals and actions are what make walking remarkable and radical. Sincerity is directly related to achieving the trust of a community and its forgiveness when there are missteps. Sincerity is what makes project mistakes forgivable.

Walking is a new form of radicalism because it not only fights and resists the neo-fascism that fears globalism, but it challenges the urban bubble of embittered liberalism that enables our disunited states of polarization. Sincerity disarms polarities and contributes to unity.

Walking requires a change of identity: from a passive, bored or distracted viewer of Internet spectacles, to an agent who refuses our obsession with cellular signals and walks into the messiness of life regardless of mobile phone range, becoming an intellectually, emotionally, and physically present participant, knowing and intuiting that this is the only way to fully perceive reality.

Sometimes we should only be engaged in one task,
and one conversation.
Sometimes we simply need to be here and only here,
in only one place at a time.

Reality abhors the negative.
Reality is intrinsically positive.
Reality is based on recycling.
Reality is pure hope.

Walking Disarmament

Thinking back about the evolution of my practice as my profession, my sense of justice has usually spoken ahead of what could be called "career strategy," undoing it right and left. If there was ever any possibility in a boardroom for my brain "to strategize" career-wise, all I needed to do was to allow the justice stored in my body to flow out of me, immediately vanishing all possibility. At first, it was embarrassing; later, I found it humorous; in the end, it became inevitable—it was ingrained; it was my practice.

Nevertheless, even when I strategized during my first decade as an artist, it was at the service of seeking an ethical state of the arts, institutionally, and artwork that addressed injustices perpetrated against individuals and groups. Over the years, my practice became more of a vessel for justice the more I detached from the illusion of me, because the illusion of the ambitiously constructed self triggers injustices around that demanding construction.

Pursuing this path, I came to the conviction that art mediums were but visual languages through which to address issues. I never sought to promote my personhood, but to promote a practice that was ultimately about justice, to support a just landscape that is part of the economy of consciousness. Of course, consciousness can be achieved in spite of and in the midst of injustice, but injustice calls forth so many negative emotions and destructive desires, like hate and revenge, that I came to believe that establishing justice created a much safer landscape for walking toward consciousness.

In fighting for justice not just during public performances but more often than not behind closed cultural doors, I have tried not to wear an impenetrable armor because this ultimately suffocates the capacity to listen. I have tried not to carry weaponry because the possession and use of psychic weapons hardens the heart. At one point, our psychic disarmament becomes nearly impossible, not only because our armor is locked, but also because there is little love left inside. Therefore, the challenge is how to avoid wearing armor and carrying arms so as to prevent a war.

However, if a cultural war becomes an unavoidable destiny, our wisdom will then consist in knowing just how much protection we need, and when and how to disarm quickly and completely so as to reveal the greatest of weapons: a forgiving heart.

Of course, there are those who are not moved by the sight of a big heart; they approach this disarmed revelation as an opportunity to destroy. Nevertheless, I always seek to disarm in public view. Indeed, my performances are invitations to collectively disarm gradually, catching glimpses of a just society, experiencing that society one project at a time.

Walking Aesthetics

For me, aesthetics are not a contaminated envelope or straightjacket. They exist somewhere in-between welcoming points of safe entry into a work and acts of generosity.

Therefore, what do you look like when you walk? Are you wearing a uniform or a costume? Is it a costume that you created as the skin of this gesture? Is it a uniform constructed as an expression of your identity in the world, which you wear every day of your life? Alternatively, is it a secret uniform to reveal your true identity, perhaps seldom revealed in the world, which you are selectively willing to reveal during a performance? (Of course, it could be a uniform to cover your identity, as you may feel too exposed.) Is it the uniform that you wear when you walk? Perhaps you wear the same uniform for every walk, regardless of site, so that it visually helps to curate (to identify, to connect) all your walking into one practice.

Sometimes I ask young performative walkers what they are going to wear during a walk they are planning. Some inevitably answer that they are "going to wear nothing special." And my reply is that "nothing special" is a uniform: it is the uniform of the unnoticed, the result of a decision to walk mostly unnoticed. In addition, and more importantly, "nothing special" is not rootless. In fact, it may be the uniform of whiteness, because there is no textile without social and cultural significance. Unnoticeability is the uniform of Americanized and Europeanized social environments, because it assumes a racially non-discriminatory, informal class structure, and gender-relaxed society. The experience of complete unnoticeability, of total freedom on a sidewalk or path, is mostly a white experience.

Of course, I understand taking on the mantle of invisibility as a strategy for research, and even for access, which may require a walker to look harmless. In addition to unnoticeability as a kind of performative camouflage, a walker may try to wear the skin of humility. True humility is admirable: it is disarming, opening many paths, and it is the first step to listening. However, to decide to be mostly unnoticeable is not automatically humble. It may be the result of thoughtlessness, or worse, the desire not to be bothered by anyone, which can be a form of avoidance of responsibility. Yet, some sites demand our courage, in the form of our visibility, to be seen to be engaged, to model engagement, if not the prophetic.

If walking is an art practice, then, I inevitably wonder about recognizable elements of form. I do not mean that walking as an art practice has to have art-historical, formal elements. Nevertheless, I seek elements that can inform and form walking as an art.

So, what is your form? Does it have a skin? Are you interested in aesthetics? What are your aesthetics? Or do you distrust and even reject aesthetic qualities? If you are eliminating all aesthetic traits from your work, then, what are you giving the viewer? Play? Does relating to play rather than relating to beauty replace aesthetics in your work? What makes the viewer approach your work from a distance? What welcomes the viewer into your work? What helps the viewer to remain inside your work? Is there a sensory difference between recruitment and engagement?

Where is your generosity? What are the visual components of your generosity? Can you reconsider beauty as an act of generosity? If not, then, please do not forget that you need to give.

Walking Ethics

Can the act of walking be justified if the walker sees nothing, if the walker contemplates nothing other than the self?

The answer depends on a list of intimate reasons.

Sometimes the self is thrown about by internal turmoil; sometimes the self is drowning in despair. Pain can make the self temporarily unable to transcend itself, unable to respond to the outside world.

Therefore, my answer to this question is affirmative, as long as the outer landscape is not in crisis or under threat of destruction.

There is also the fact that those blinded by grief often find sight along the very path that they could not see. Because the path saw them.

Sometimes, walking a path of destruction for the sake of our own survival wakes us up to the need to walk for the survival of others. There is no retroactive Adam and Eve. We realize that our individual survival depends on our collective survival.

Sometimes, walking a path self-absorbed, initially experiencing nothing but the novice's effort to control our breath and our breathlessness, is what eventually opens our sight. What started as breathing practice becomes seeing—the practice of sight. The more our breath comes under control, the more our mind is free to see.

So, it is best not to rush to judge a walk by its beginnings. It is best to wait to evaluate a walk by its results. Because beginnings are often imperfect, for the wrong reason, moving wrong, in the wrong direction.

There is an arc to learning how to walk. The ethics of a walker are best appreciated after much walking. That is why we must practice—walking. Because the path itself teaches us how to walk, for what reasons, and in what direction.

The path holds the ethics of the practice.

Walking the Imagination

Terms are contaminated and thus burdened by the gendered history of manipulative power. Nevertheless, because I work with communities to whom I need to describe a project using accessible, clear language, I try to rescue words from this ruined landscape of historic speech, reclaiming original meanings or redefining them.

I want to believe that we can rescue imagination, that is, our understanding of the purpose and agency of imagination in society. I am aware that we live in an age where we mistakenly think that we have the right to fully access and consume everything, even the stories of others. However, I believe that this can be curated by ethics.

Therefore, I define a *moral imagination* as the ability to imagine yourself in someone else's shoes. An *ethical imagination* is the ability to imagine yourself wearing those shoes—inhabiting them—walking through the world as another person. It is not enough to stand like a lightning rod; it is necessary to inhabit and walk in place of.

Inhabiting and walking in someone else's shoes begins to generate a *radical imagination*, that is, an imagination at its most productive, socially heroic and prophetic.

Walking Language

I am not a supporter of art theory as the only nutrient for art training. I received a Western European education in the humanities by way of Spain, complemented by the pre-Columbian and colonial literature of the Caribbean, Central and South America, updated by Cold War violations on the neo-colonial stages of Cuba and Puerto Rico, followed by the African-American struggle for civil rights, white feminist theory, and queer movement documentation. I continue to be humbly schooled, most recently in the perversion of globalism by forces such as unrestrained capitalism, invasive technology masquerading as social media, and the populist neo-fascism of a post-industrial, angry underclass that feels betrayed. Of course, not everything is negative schooling, and there are global ecological restoration initiatives (even if fought by big oil and gas), and inspiring local efforts at artisanal organic farming, and the rebirth of farmer networks. They may not feed a world that should not be overpopulated in the first place, and that also wastes a lot of food, but they are slowly making food production real again. This trajectory continues to homeschool me as a multidisciplinary thinker and maker; it informed my thinking through contradictory theories which made me suspect the authority of any single theory.

I also seek the knowledge deeply stored within the human body, the possibility of distant memory fragments passed through our DNA, and more recent muscle memories often related to the experience of pain. I seek to understand perception through our known senses, plus intuition and instinct. Not harboring the prejudices of secular modernity, I also desire to be informed by the human spirit as a self-less, empathic receiver. The perceptual result of all this is vital to walking practice.

If given a choice, I prefer to walk rather than to theorize about walking. Nevertheless, after I walk and rest from walking, I eventually begin to think about the experience of walking, and frequently write my wandering reflections. Moreover, because a new generation of artists is increasingly walking as socially engaged art practice, I formulate some of these reflections in the multidisciplinary language of the times; and because academic, art theoretical terminology has failed to give artists working in the field a generous, descriptive language for documenting their emotional experiences, particularly when they challenge secular modernity.

There is no question that art theory has given artists the tools with which to decode authoritarian systems. But until recently, theory had been unable to provide a terminology that accurately describes artists' sincere, generous, performative field exchanges, as they used the arts as responsive, aesthetic methodologies, ethically addressing visible and invisible, complex issues for human and non-human animals and their environments. Contemporary artists urgently need a new language to generate individual and collective, cathartic and transformative experiences that are socially useful, in terms of village-value as opposed to art world-value, contributing to a healed culture of consciousness.

Contemporary artists should not be imprisoned within art theoretical language but should be set free to borrow language from all disciplines, as long as this borrowing is about revolutionizing their making. Otherwise, this interdisciplinary borrowing merely employs non-art-making language in order to keep making socially irrelevant images and objects.

In addition to problems around communicating field experience, there is also a problem in evaluating it. In this respect, art cannot continue to be self-referential regarding cultural practices such as walking that were originally not art-making practices. A cultural process cannot be solely judged as an art process, because it is too limited, because culture is bigger than art.

Non-art-making practices have different histories, carry different theoretical languages, and produce forms and inventories beyond historic art materials, art mediums, art styles, and art content increasingly amassed in excessive, unsustainable museum, gallery, and private collection storage. (Perhaps some folks need to start performing not in galleries, but in art storage units.) We should thank the universe for finally living in an age where an art form (walking) does not produce more clutter but more experience.

Ultimately, I believe that the language of walking as art practice is already here, active and operating among us but scattered throughout many other discourses. Therefore, it only needs to be identified, harvested, threaded, and revealed by our first steps. Perhaps in doing so, art may stop being such an elitist big business with such a small social presence.

When I write of walking practice as art practice that joins cultural practice, it is not in the conventional sense, but in the sense that I am going to borrow terminology from the language of non-art-making disciplines such as ecology, ethnography, psychology, and Zen Buddhist studies, in order to quilt a new multidisciplinary discourse of walking as art practice leading to conscious cultural production. My hope is that this discourse strikes everyone as not new but, in fact, as embarrassingly obvious. Walking practice has always been there, within reach, like Buddha's notion of enlightenment, already within us, only a matter of arms-length awareness.

Walking Leadership

There are positive and negative forms of leadership. Leading a group of walkers while constantly talking like a tour guide, leaving no room for silence, can block the subtle sounds of the natural world. This may also result in only regarding the most obvious features of a landscape, noticing only what a chatty group leader points to as notable. This not only filters everyone's perceptions according to a busy leader's menu, but also creates a walking audience that inwardly organizes itself hierarchically. A leader needs to avoid the creation of a negative hierarchy bookended by needy followers who compete for a leader's undivided attention, to walkers lagging behind, fighting the experience because they have issues with authority, and the in-between, who try to stay out of this dysfunctional walking dynamic.

Some older children and adolescent participants may have been dragged into the walk very much against their will by parents or guardians. Some adult participants signed up perhaps not realizing what they were getting into because they did not read the project literature or because they did not comprehend it. Of course, sometimes a project wants to surprise, so its literature does not say much. That can be tricky, and can backfire.

Some people do not want to be led anywhere. I like to find my own way because I seek or notice what most dismiss. I am a group leader but I identify with those who do not wish to follow. Even though I have led many a museum tour, I never take museum tours. I like to encounter cultural artifacts on my own. However, when entrusted with leading a walk, I need all to follow, no matter my empathy with the resistant.

Some walking projects require pedagogical leadership, particularly when the walkers are foreign to a landscape, or when the walkers have lost their connection to their landscape and need to reacquaint themselves with it through a walking artist who is trying to facilitate their experience of it anew. This can become a test, of course, as some of the locally-born-and-raised may examine the artist walker, scrutinizing every step. However, we need to embrace the fact that grassroots folks have the inalienable right to test us. This is where humility comes in; the artist walker must walk into a landscape as a permeable entity willing to do all it takes to earn people's respectful trust.

The most meaningful collective walks are those in which all walkers have done their homework, are perceptive, open to the unexpected, and walk quietly and unhurriedly, for the sake of listening and seeing, only selectively sharing insights with each other, if and when appropriate, along the way or after the walk. Waiting for after a walk is sometimes best. Not everything has to be shared on the spot. The social media cult of instant sharing and commenting, immediately turning everything into a post on a constantly updated timeline of likes and dislikes, can kill the state of deep perception.

Walking requires a methodology of generosity. It is important that walkers watch each other, and watch out for each other, as part of a path's emotionally mature ecology. This is not about supervision. A walk's leader is in charge of supervision. No other walker needs to supervise his or her fellow walkers. In fact, unless the leader appoints one or more assistants, based on scholarship, experience, or skills, the leader must discourage self-appointed supervisors, either through discretion or through a clear public statement that empowers everyone equally.

A walk's leader must embrace authority. Otherwise, a walking group can become fragmented and the walking experience can deteriorate quickly. There should be clear guidelines. Even when a group experience seeks to embrace diversity of individual experience, in terms of different decisions and expressions during moments of intimacy with the self, these, too, must be at the service of the collective. All individual performer decisions and gestures will take place within the context of the group and will reflect upon the group.

There is no question that a walk's leader wants to perceive, too. A walk's group leader wants to experience the path as much as the walk's participants. But this is where leadership requires sacrifice and generosity. Like a lead performance artist who holds the space for other performers, a walk's leader must hold the path for others. This means that a group leader needs to nourish his/her own perception before and after a group walk.

I always walk my group's path alone before and after their walk. It is not only about evaluation and preparation. If a path is fragile, the walk turns me into a gatekeeper. In certain cases, I may need to open a path so that my group may enter. Later, I may need to close the path after my group exists.

The above is quite prescriptive, of course, but nothing is carved into stone. I encourage everyone to develop their walking methodologies, clearly expressed through written guidelines for site-specific contexts, knowing when to stand firm and when to adapt them flexibly, or discard them altogether and start anew. But if a performative walking practice as art has been developed and tested over years, there are a core set of skills and tools that strike at the heart of the human condition and are gently transferrable, from project to project. These walking skills and tools can be a strong thread that unites all of a walker's projects, from site to site, ranging from a curatorial signature to a common human value or cause because we are One.

Walking Rejections

Sometimes I want to walk somewhere and request resources, but doors close to my eagerness of step and means do not materialize. Rejection is particularly hard for a young walker. It can feel like being cast indefinitely into the prison of stasis.

How do we transform stasis into stillness?

There is a message in rejection, but it is not necessarily the message conveyed by those who rejected me. It is more of an intimate, barely audible whisper for the core of me. Rejection is an invitation to slowness, reflection, and redirection.

When someone rejects my walk, I do not cease to walk but I slow down to a pause. I see it as an invitation to pause reflectively. It may not be the invitation I wanted, but it is the one received. Therefore, by slowing my steps and reflecting, I begin to engage in a meditative stillness.

I am not afraid of stillness, for in stillness I walk invisibly. I walk an invisible cartography: the emotional map of rejection, because I must know the full range of my feelings and ultimately detach from negative feeling; the political map of institutional rejection, because I must try to understand current curatorial preferences, even if I disagree with them; and the invisible map of vision, because perhaps I was walking in the wrong direction. Perhaps I must embrace the fact that walking practice as art is prophetic, beyond the fashion of the times, walking solitarily in a different direction.

A nondestructive impediment is but a form of existential curation. In addition, even when I get to physically walk in the material world, with funding, I am but remembering my walk.

Let me explain.

I have a notion of time that often drives me to write and say that I make work as one who has already died. I am ultimately detached from my proposals, no matter how passionately I write them, because I believe that I am long gone. Yet, someone is remembering me, someone is remembering our project. The project is but a meaningful memory that we are going to revisit together.

In this detached line of thought, the question is not how am I going to make a work of art, but how are we going to remember a transformative experience together? What do we want to remember? Do we want to remember something that was competitive and successful, or something that was communal and transformative?

Approaching the future through memory gives me a unique opportunity. Instead of being anxiously ahead of myself, I am already done and my choice is not about the professional achievement of successful art authorship, but about contributing to conscious experience through art.

Walking Slowness

Walking slowly can counteract our addiction to speed, our individual and collective cult of speed, which dulls all senses. We now fear slowness as lack of wit, evidencing less intelligence. The slow are suspect. The village idiot is slow; the town's fool drags his feet. But who wrote that story? Who created that cruel cartoon? Certainly not a walker.

Monastic cultures are wisely slow. The monastic body trains in the craft of slowness.

Americans fear slowness as a loss of momentum. Business is all about the rhythms of timing and grabbing. However, what if there is another layer to timing? What if there is a supra-human timing? What if we walked slowly and, by the very virtue of our slowness, could see and hear much more? What if our slowness allowed us to encounter slow and subtle entities missed by speed?

What if there is a *psychic timing*? What if our psychic acuity can only perceive an unseen, slowly unfolding, deeper environment through slowness? What if it requires the sum of our known senses, intuition and instinct, and the human spirit as an organ of perception, all combined? It takes time to gather and unite as one, internally; our internal oneness cannot be rushed. And what if this psychic timing choreographs us to exit our homes at just the right time, to enter paths at just the right moment, in order to experience a rare natural event that we are meant to see and hear, or to encounter another human animal, or a non-human animal, to know and to become known by, in order to connect with and without words?

What if everything and everyone is being choreographed by this greater collective psychic timing in universal flow, which may not have a choreographer other than the elements in the process and the process itself, once unleashed (the big bang?). I do not know; I do not need to know. For me, for my walk, what suffices is the need to be aware of it, so as to flow into and connect with others within it, becoming one.

Many people are afraid that if they slow down, they will never recover their prior speed. Many fear that they might remain slow forever, and thus, stuck in a permanent perceptual disadvantage across the industrial and post-industrial worlds. There is so much fear of the slow unknown.

We cannot let our walking art practice be curated by speed. We cannot let our walking practice be dictated by fear of slowness. Walking unknown paths requires trust in the nourishing of the yet-unknown, and in the very concept of the unknown itself.

To know what we do not know is important to knowing, to the quality of our knowledge, giving it perspective and depth, giving it subtlety and wisdom. This process is not a race; this is a very slow evolution, an evolved knowledge of our universal ignorance, very slowly achieved, wisely discerned.

Walking Teachers

My father loved taking long car rides on week-nights to the city's outskirts. I remember driving by a petrochemical refinery, along kilometers that paralleled shiny metallic tubing, drum-like storage domes, tall towers with open flames, and toxic fumes. I could barely breathe even as all our car windows were closed, the filtering air conditioning collapsing. The landscape resembled a *Star Wars* set, a science fiction inferno, and the meadows and hills around it were barren, like a place that was clawed into a wasteland. Some of the most haunting rides of my life have been at night, sitting quietly with my younger brother in the back of dad's car, looking through glass while listening to his favorite singers: Harry Belafonte, Nat King Cole, Sammy Davis Jr., and Charles Aznavour, whose deep smooth voice still echoes through my ears. The city's modern, wide throughways became surreal in the dark, like smooth, hard rivers of cement and concrete tinted by yellowish streetlights and whitish fluorescents, punctuated by red and green traffic lights. I can close my eyes and still see those images, vividly. On weekends, dad would drive us far beyond, into open sunny countryside, and on through towns and villages, stopping by the side of the road for fruits and juice.

My mother was my first walking teacher. She loved to take long walks across the city, and brought me along to keep her company, to ward off unsolicited male attention (she was a very elegant, beautiful woman), and to help carry her shopping bags. Mom walked with determination, looking at everything and everyone, not missing anything as an intelligent observer. Because she was a well-known school principal, we stopped often to talk with the parents of her students. It was like walking around with the city's mayor. Over the years, my mother became unable to walk because of arthritis of the feet and spinal damage. It was a huge blow to how we related. When I visit her nowadays, my octogenarian mother and I choose a location, and we drive there together. She sits on a bench, encouraging me to let her be and take a walk. She wants me to walk, and to watch me walk. So, I walk away, as she watches me closely. As I later walk back, she watches me as I perform for her the walk she can no longer do.

I have experienced many teachers. Most did not know they were teaching me about walking, but some did it consciously. Curator Saralyn Reece Hardy knowingly taught me how to see and listen to the Midwest, introducing me to Willa Cather, whose fiction I devoured. Saralyn was a jackrabbit of a fast walker; I could barely keep up with her. I also remember visiting The Land Institute with her, trying to keep up with its founder Wes Jackson, a former McArthur Fellow and author of *Becoming Native to This Place*. By then, he was an Abrahamic octogenarian who walked ahead with hurried, giant steps to show me the wide grooves left by the mythical wagon wheels of the homesteaders, like deep, dry, mud gullies etched over 100 years ago. He was testing me to see if I was strong enough to walk across his mythical landscape. Lifelong bird watcher Marge Streckfuss and her friend, senior botanist Iralee Barnard, walked me across stretches of the Tall Grass Prairie Preserve and showed me homestead ruins and American bison wallows. However, it was poet Lori Brack who taught me some of the most important lessons of them all: that the prairie is inhabited by massive bodies with gentle voices and that Kansas women speak like the wind. Experiencing Kansas was like being caught in a windstorm that swept me up into the air and blew me across the Midwest, providing me with incredible vistas. I sometimes think that I have not landed yet.

In Utah, a group of Mormon and ex-Mormon women artists of all ages, gatekeepers of that psychic landscape, opened invisible paths so that I could walk the visible but see the invisible. In Puerto Rico, a young woman opened up a deep night with embedded corner entities that had been blocking our project, recruiting me to secretly dispel them through Yoruba spells during a scary, landscape-healing walk. Art school certainly never trained me for that. In Hawaii, native women artists revealed a landscape hidden in plain sight, parting invisible curtains so that I could walk with them and truly see their islands. All these sited women, people-of-place were the most haunting, unforgettable teachers I have ever had.

These days, I have non-human teachers. I have lived with herding dogs for the past 20 years. Herders are about finding and following scent down a trail, so they have taught me to walk from a non-human perspective. Herders are also about herding groups into shape and moving them through challenging territories into shelter. Dogs have been some of my most revealing teachers, teaching me how non-humans move across terrain. We need more movement perspectives than the anthropocentric.

Who are your human and non-human teachers? We should remember and record our histories of walking. It is a writing exercise I have often assigned to my graduate students during master workshops. Write your personal history of walking.

Body Knowledge

I do not know how to teach the knowledge of the body except through anecdote. My body teachings consist of a string of stories in which the body knows ahead of the brain. The brain is only an element of the mind. The body is the mind too.

I have a friend whose only son died at the age of 35 from a heart attack. He began to have chest pains and died in his mother's arms by the side of the road, on their way to a regular doctor's appointment. His parents cremated the body and dispersed his ashes privately. However, they held a community memorial, to which I was invited. It took place on a very cold Saturday afternoon in mid-December, inside a Quaker Meeting House in the middle of a beautiful hayfield.

I decided to walk there from my house. I could have driven my truck; I could have ridden my bike. Though my brain was puzzled, concerned about the distance and the cold, my body chose to walk because it wanted to approach slowly, on foot. My body decided that the gesture of walking was how I should honor him.

I realize the challenge is describing this moment, because verbal language was made by the brain. Words are the terms of the brain. Gestures are the terms of the body. If the body acts without the brain's blessing, it has "decided" to act. The body has made a decision. The decision did not come from the brain (the intellect). But that does not mean that it was visceral. The mind is in the body as much as in the brain. (The mind is in the toe as much as in the head.) The mind decides through the body, without the brain. You might say that in a complex urgent situation, the mind is able to take a shortcut through the body. In that sense, the body can make perfectly intelligent decisions without thought, because it is responding to something greater than the brain, it is acting for the mind.

So the day arrived, and I bundled up and began walking to the field, making my way down the forested, hilly topography around my house, observing trees and mossy rocks, enjoying the bright winter light but surprised by all the garbage along the side of the road.

As I said before, my brain could not explain it, but my body needed to walk there, to arrive walking even if no one saw me. Indeed, no one did, for everyone was already inside by the time I got there. The service had just begun as I sat at the back of the room and listened to his family and friends speak of how my friend's son loved to walk, of how he took buses and walked long distances.

Unlike many others in the room, I only knew his mother; I never met him during his lifetime. Somehow, my body knew him. My body was in tune with something about a life nearby that was suddenly lost, but whose energetic residue was still around us, walking.

Writing About Walking

When I think of the basic requirements for walking, I believe that, more than legs, walking requires communication, verbal and nonverbal languages.

English is my second language. As a child, I attended a bilingual school and was required to study English in primary school, but I initially rejected it. It was not until high school that my second language became a door to modernity and a window to globalism. Modernity and globalism are complex states and forces that I have deconstructed and criticized as an adult, but there is no question that I accessed them through this second language. However, I do not consider myself a good writer because I do not have enough vocabulary in this language.

I love words but I do not know all the words in English. Knowing this limitation but nevertheless driven to write, I try to write from a different vantage point: a lyrical vulnerability. Every time I approach writing, I seek to strip myself of all weapons and armor to write about what is hard to express: what is secret, emotional, and embarrassing; what is intellectually suspicious. I try to write with an unguarded heart; I try to write with sincerity.

Sincerity, defined as the quality of being open and truthful in a straightforward way, free from pretense, is currently discredited, perhaps because we are undergoing a pretentious moment in which all writing, even artists' writings, are required to be backed by inventories of theories as the only form of credibility. As an artist, I find this unacceptable because I believe in our capacity as creative individuals to generate original thought as triggered by meaningful experiences. Yet, it is as if conceptualism, as the ruling form of academic training, has eliminated all possible competitors for the act of creation, dismissing our deepest emotions and our rawest experiences, accepting reshuffled bibliographies as the only equation for creation.

We have lost sight of what true originality means. In the United States, this is killing American artists and American art, creating institutionalized artists and textbook art. It is as if there were a degree-awarding troll in a tollbooth at the end of an expensive graduate speedway. The troll at the toll will send you back if you do not arrive with the one standardized formula. The troll does not ask for prophetic vision and social agency.

It may read as disingenuous for me to have spent two decades as an educator, and then seem to dump on academic theses and theoretical bibliographies. However, these were never meant to become what solely defined a visual artist's education for society. This state of the arts is the result of standardizing art education within American universities and colleges, while also increasing its costs. Artists should be eclectic readers and well-trained technicians, but emotion and experience are what balance and complete our ability to have social agency.

Early on, I decided not to teach until much later in life, so that by then I would have field experiences to bring into the classroom. But even then, I decided to be only a part-time instructor so as to constantly come up for oxygen. Throughout my 20 years in classrooms, my understanding of training remained the facilitation of perceptual and expressive skills rather than theorizing.

One may miss the vision of a horizon because of the minutiae of a landscape's intricate geology, forever detained by what has come before, to the point of becoming unable to move on by accessing one's own vision. There is something perverse when education squelches individual vision by requiring us to inventory everyone else's visions, to the point that a young artist's still-fragile vision is diminished and lost to insecurity. I have spent countless hours walking through MFA studios trying to access and give courage to young artists' visions. Sometimes, I feel as if original thought, based solely on its own merit, is not allowed. Insecurity is a systemic problem among our micromanaged graduate art students.

I still believe in risking writing from experience, about experience. Growing up, I spent many hours writing, but my teachers paid little attention to it. Perhaps they were not writers. But I was also an unattractive little brown boy. The well dressed, pretty white boys were the ones who got all the attention, no matter how badly they behaved. Only once, in junior high, after writing a particularly passionate composition, did our teacher mention in passing that I wrote well. That crumb of a comment meant the world to me after a little lifetime of invisibility. It was not until university that my writing efforts received any recognition and guidance.

As a child, I wanted to study many fields. I wanted to be an archaeologist or geologist (because I was fascinated by ruins and stones); I was enamored with the notion of being park ranger (out of a desire to be alone in Nature); I thought of becoming a veterinarian (feeling an overwhelming compassion for animals); I pursued studies in sociology and psychology (as I was attracted to society and the human mind); even as I also secretly desired to be an actor, a dancer, and a singer (driven to creative self-expression). I dreamed of being a writer, too. Of all the practices I admired, writing actually seemed to contain aspects from them all: observation, solitude, empathy, scholarliness, and creative communication. In fact, it appeared to be the most sustainable. Writing seemed like something one could do well into old age. But I did not become a full-time professional writer. I became an artist who seeks languages through which to communicate my walking experiences, even as walking is a language, too.

I think that all walkers should consider writing about walking, because paths give us a vocabulary, verbal and nonverbal, literary and physical, which eventually amounts to a holistic language, to the generous language of walking.

Postscript: *Onwards*

I remember the first time I visited the Kansas prairie in the year 2000. Saralyn Reece Hardy, then director of the Salina Art Center and later director of the Spencer Art Museum at the University of Kansas, brought me west to visit her land and walk with her people. We remain in touch with each other and, when I told her about this book, she wrote: "To walk is to believe in something."

I believe that walking as socially engaged practice is gaining followers. For example, the Walk Exchange was founded in 2010 in Brooklyn by a group of artists and citizens, among them, Bess Matasa, the first woman to ride the entire New York City subway system over 24 uninterrupted hours, and Dillon de Give, an alum of the MFA in Social Practice at Portland State University. Dillon is known for his Coyote Walks, retracing the often-tragic route of wildlife making incursions into NYC. The Exchange offers creative walks and annual training.

In 2014, Deveron Projects' director, Claudia Zeiske, founded The Walking Institute in the market town of Huntly, Scotland. Claudia recruits artistic bodies to choreograph considered walking experiences in her region. That same year, artist Angela Ellsworth co-founded The Museum of Walking at Arizona State University, in Tempe, a city whose desert weather makes it challenging to walk for most of the year. MoW has a modest but growing archive and library of walking materials, and has become an originator of regional walking programming. In January 2017, we witnessed one of the largest marches in Washington in recent US history, accompanied by sister marches worldwide. Hundreds of thousands of women walked peacefully seeking protection for their rights.

More and more art schools are offering walking seminars and workshops as electives for young artists interested in socially engaged art practice. More and more mature, established artists are coming out of the closet with their intimate walking practices, once kept private as part of their creative processes. Well known multimedia artist Leslie Dill, with whom I performed *Labor of*

Love at the Noguchi Museum in 2014, recently shared the following: "When I prepare to walk, I start with a meditative pause to locate myself in the feeling of the space, a growing feeling as my feet get connected to the ground. I adjust my pelvis. I breathe. I wait. And then I start. My body moves slowly but inevitably into trance. I become fully aware of the soles of my feet. I become hyper-aware of the floor. The floor is no longer separate from my psyche. The floor becomes the back of a huge animal, like a gigantic elephant. My feet now walk in tenderness, giving solace to the back of the titan. I become love, infinite."

German performance artist Lisa Stertz with whom I travelled to Japan in 2016, shares her recent discovery of Baguazhang, a 19th-century practice combining Chinese martial arts with Daoism based on circular motions and circle-walking, clockwise and counterclockwise. Seeking stillness of mind, Lisa walks a circle slowly, under the sky, seeking to connect with the ground. She speaks of how she can walk a great distance, never leaving the place in spite of the length of her walk, a walk that replenishes rather than depletes her because it never allows her to walk away from her strong inner core, always keeping it at the center of her awareness.

For performance artist Sara Jimenez, walking creates a space for intimacy. In a series of e-mail exchanges, she shared that "Growing up, my family had dinner every evening together. Our dinners were always rushed and strained. The feeling of being together tended to be overwhelming. Yet, after dinner, my father would always ask if we wanted to go for a walk. It would be dusk, the sky a pale white, yellow and pink, with gnats buzzing in the air. We would all walk together. Sometimes it would be the long walk, up the hill. Sometimes it would be the short walk, just around the block. In this moment of intimacy, moving side by side, we channeled our energy through our bodies, through movement. We were able to talk about things that would be too intense to address sitting inside and looking at each other across the table. Difficult topics had space to float to the surface. Walking allowed our conversations to be tempered, our issues acknowledged."

Sara also reflected on how intimacy can often have a public life, whether walkers are aware of it or not. She went on to share that "When I was a little girl, my father would walk me to school every day. I attended the same school from age five to 17. He would walk me there on the way to work. When I was five, he would carry my red tote bag, which had a sequined princess on the surface, sewn by my mother. When I was a teenager, my father would insist on helping me carry my large backpack full of books. Every morning we spent about 20 minutes together, the space between our home and my school. Sometimes we connected during the walks; other times we fought. But that path was ours; it was where we could grow together, side by side, imperfectly. One evening, my father came home and told me that he had a funny experience. A stranger had walked up to him on the subway and said, 'On my commute to work, I have seen you and your daughter walk to school every day for the past 10 years. I feel like I have witnessed her growing up. I just wanted to let you know.' The walk had not only been our private moment together, but had also become a way of marking time as a public ritual, a connection to a larger community."

Educator Carol Padberg, the founder of a new, experimental MFA program in interdisciplinary art which takes its graduate students into the field, visiting model artist community projects nationwide, recently moved her family into inner city Hartford, Connecticut, so as to live what she teaches. Carol walks daily through her poor neighborhood and writes: "Through concrete and asphalt, my feet convey a message to the soil below. I swap emotions and breath with the boulevard's trees. Every walk is a nature walk. Last week found me dreaming up the future, house-by-house and block-by-block— one where the children and the earth are top priority. The sidewalk on my block spans vacant lots. Further down, there is a burnt-out apartment complex. Some walks feel solitary, as I can get lost in my thoughts. Yet, most walks are remarkably social. I send and receive. I find pairs of eyes and greet my new family: a dad, an auntie, a brother, a son—myself. It is a brief encounter, maybe with a few words, or through meaningful silence."

Artist Erin Sweeny has been walking since 2014 in an ongoing project called *Good Fridays*, which began with a 26-mile walk from Santa Fe, New Mexico, to El Santuario de Chimayo. Erin is engaged in a continuing investigation of walking and race, gender, space, and ritual. She engages in walking practice as a way to witness, document, and come to understand a place. In spring 2017, she walked the 13-mile route between Battery Park and Inwood Hill Park in New York City, inviting friends and colleagues to join her all the way, or part of the way.

I read performance artist Hannah Barco's prose poem, *Making Bread Out of Nothing*, and like a child picking through a rich plate of food, I pick at her performative instructions for they hide the recipe of a walk: "Does all of your weight shift to one side or the other? If I gave you a shove, would you fall? Next time a waiter brings a basket of bread to your table, wrap it in a napkin, stick it in your pocket, and ask for more. Be stubborn…" and then, "Wrap yourself in a blanket and go for a walk." She writes, "While walking, pay attention to what each person carries with them." Because, "Our bodies know so much more than we imagine." She asks, "What did you leave behind, when you went out for that walk?" Remember, "If you get hungry, there's some bread in your pocket." Hannah walks forcefully, like a Midwestern farmer's wife, carrying the frame of a house and its entire household on her strong back into an uncertain American future. But I will never lack for bread if Hannah is walking performatively ahead of me, because the future belongs to her steps. She is kneading the future with her toes.

In Puerto Rico, devastated by hurricane Maria in 2017, artist Mari Mater O'Neill, in partnership with Sara Marina Dorna, has been engaged in a series of walks since 2014, trekking and hiking throughout their island, mapping trails and documenting their experiences. O'Neill began to walk seriously in Western Europe, during her doctoral studies, first in the UK and later in Spain, along the Camino de Santiago de Compostela. Mari continued after her return to San Juan, realizing that there was little information about long-distance walking across Puerto Rico. Three years later, Mari's and Sara's walks have been documented in a remarkable publication, *Current Landscape*. Their publication is a wonderfully hybrid text, part guide, part journal, and part manifesto. It does not seek the neo-colonizing tourist scanning of topography. The authors share their walking practice and invite you to walk a landscape that was often dismissed in the colonial past, was recently ravaged by a catastrophic hurricane, but remains surprisingly resilient and rich.

All of these institutions and groups, mature and young artists, some of them former students, constitute my partners and peers on the road, and my inspiration to keep walking. This small artist book belongs to them.

Glossary

A selection of key terms, as I define and use them throughout this book.

Awareness – Awareness is often confused with consciousness. I define awareness as the basic state of being informed about someone or something.

Charrette – A small group meeting seeking a balanced dialogue about selected common issues, giving voice to all participants and focusing on creative solutions.

Civilization – Historically, a powerful people and their leading culture, traditionally constructed and sustained through material and psychological domination. Ideally, a people's evolved state, best evidenced through their awareness of all sentient beings' rights.

Conscious – The conscious is our system for becoming and staying human in the animal world through the formulation of ideas communicated through language and images.

Contemplation – The deep(er) consideration of thoughts, for a long period, with an element of surrender.

Docents – A term commonly used in museums for mature volunteers trained to speak with visitors about exhibitions and performances.

Hyper-Awareness – A heightened state of awareness; a precondition to consciousness.

Meditation – The rumination on ideas, resulting in considered thoughts.

Mind – The totality of the self. Mind combines thoughts and ideas with feelings and emotions (the so-called heart), plus memories stored in organs (the visceral), fiber and muscle. The mind is not sited only in the brain. The mind is as much in the finger and toe as in the brain.

Nature & nature – I capitalize Nature when I envision the contextual environment as a living entity and influential force, as opposed to the lower-case nature of something or someone, and human nature.

No-Thought – Christianity walks the mind from reflection, through meditation, to contemplation. Buddhism seems to go one step further: it takes the mind to no-thought, quieting the mind, willingly surrendering all thinking to a peaceful oblivion that does not negate or destroy the self, but simply suspends it, giving it a taste of the silence and flow of the cosmos.

Novice – In Western monasticism, a young person seeking to become a monk or nun; someone in the early stages of monastic training. In many monasteries, it is preceded by being a Postulant, one who asks to become a Novice, usually for one year. The novitiate usually lasts for one or two years.

Practice – Most people think of a doctor's or a lawyer's practice. However, the art world did not borrow this term from these professions but from Buddhism and its notion of meditation practice. Artists are trying to move away from the influence of competitive corporate culture that has increasingly defined art as an abrasive urban career. Artists are trying to replace this with the humbler notion of art as a practice, as a mindful way of life, consisting of consciously creative gestures, visible and invisible, large and small. Art practice is a private and public, selfless and generous, creative life process resulting in a conscious cultural product.

Reflection – The act of considering events, issues, and ideas—seriously.

Socially Engaged – As I state in the beginning of this text, a socially engaged, public performance practice is the site-specific embodiment of urgent social issues through considered human gesture, such as conscious walking, ethically made and generously shared with people as a form of diagnostic, collective, poetic portrait, freely offered for aesthetic appreciation and meaningful reflection, ultimately seeking a socially transformative, cultural experience.

Unconscious & Subconscious – Many define the unconscious and the subconscious identically, considering the unconscious and the subconscious as practically interchangeable terms. However, psychoanalytic practice prefers to use the unconscious as the term for the deeper mind. Novelist Cormack McCarthy writes in his article "The Kelulé Problem" that the unconscious was our biological system for operating as an animal, which lingers as a primeval system integral to our mind. For him, the unconscious remains mostly inaccessible to the conscious and communicates with it primarily through dream sequences and images (visions), which we have to interpret. Nevertheless, throughout this book, I use the term unconscious as an *adjective*, as the opposite of conscious, meaning: insensitive or unaware. Thus, I beg to differ with common usage. The subconscious does not work for me as an adjective. Contrary to psychoanalytic usage, I prefer to use the term "subconscious" as a noun, as the name of the deeply rooted, primeval system McCarthy writes about.

References

I have always been an eclectic reader. This is an informal, alphabetized list of the authors and book titles (unless otherwise indicated) that I reference, plus other titles that have also informed my walking practice.

Pride and Prejudice by Jane Austen

Jane Eyre by Charlotte Brontë

The Snow Queen by Michael Cunningham

The Graveyard Book by Neil Gaiman

Words Without Music: A Memoir by Philip Glass

Wandering with Sadhus: Ascetics in the Hindu Himalayas by Sondra L. Hausner

Trickster Makes this World: Mischief, Myth, and Art by Lewis Hyde

Becoming Native to This Place by Wes Jackson

The Dirty Life, A Memoire of Farming, Food, and Love by Kristin Kimball

Beatrix Potter, A Life in Nature by Linda Lear

The Lure of the Local: Sense of Place in a Multicentered Society by Lucy Lippard

"The Kelulé Problem: Where did language come from?" an article by Cormack McCarthy

Sissinghurst, An Unfinished History by Adam Nicolson

The Smell of Summer Grass by Adam Nicolson

Current Landscape: Walking Across Puerto Rico by Maria de Mater O'Neill & Sara Marina Dorna

The Shepherd's Life: Modern Dispatches from an Ancient Landscape by James Rebanks

"Diary: In Fukushima," an article by Rebecca Solnit

Wanderlust, A History of Walking by Rebecca Solnit

Regarding the Pain of Others by Susan Sontag

Zen Mind, Beginners Mind by Shunryu Suzuki

The Hidden Life of Trees: What They Feel and How They Communicate—Discoveries from a Secret World by Peter Wohlleben

A Bigger Picture, a documentary by Bruno Wollheim

Orlando by Virginia Woolf

Supplementary List:

Losing Helen by Carol Becker

Spider Speculations by Jo Carson

My Antonia by Willa Cather

Freedom and Culture by John Dewey

The Chalice and the Blade: Our History, Our Future by Riane Eisler

The Earth Has a Soul by C. G. Jung

Psychology and the East by C. G. Jung

Playing in the Dark: Whiteness and the Literary Imagination by Toni Morrison

How to Walk by Thich Nhat Hanh

Mourning Sex: Performing Public Memories by Peggy Phelan

The Shepherd's View: Modern Photographs from an Ancient Landscape by James Rebanks

The Body in Pain by Elaine Scarry

New York City Trees, A Field Guide for the Metropolitan Area by Edward Sibley Barnard

A Field Guide for Getting Lost by Rebecca Solnit

The Flâneur by Edmund White

Here is New York by E. B. White

Woman is an Island by Judith Williamson

Forest Forensics by Tom Wessels

"Street Haunting: A London Adventure," an essay by Virginia Woolf

About the Author

Ernesto Pujol is a site-specific, public, performance artist and social choreographer, as well as a writer and educator. In the 1970s, he pursued undergraduate work in the humanities, art, and philosophy. During the 1980s, he sought Western monastic training in a Cistercian-Trappist cloister, followed by social work among the homeless, graduate work in education, psychology, and communications. He also served in public health addressing HIV/AIDS in the US and Latin America, as a consultant to nonprofit organizations such as the Brooklyn AIDS Task Force and GMHC in New York, the Academy for Educational Development in Washington, DC, and the Panos Institute in London. During the 1990s, Pujol began to practice socially engaged art through a series of installation projects in Cuba and Puerto Rico. In 2000, he began to collaborate with citizen curators on regional, long-term projects in the Midwest and the South. In 2011, The Contemporary (art museum) in Honolulu hosted a partial retrospective of his work and commissioned a citywide, durational performance, *Speaking in Silence.* Pujol continues to serve as a graduate studio and thesis advisor to several programs, lead field-training, master workshops, and develop group performances as public portraits of embattled people and places.

Also from Triarchy Press

Walking Stumbling Limping Falling – Alyson Hallett & Phil Smith
Two walking-authors/artists, suddenly unable to walk normally, reflect on prostheses, waddling, Butoh, built-up shoes, pain, bad legs, vertigo, hubris, bad walks, walking carefully... From their conversation emerges an Alphabet of Falling, a sustained reflection on the loss of normal capacity, and a larger discussion about stumbling and falling.

Ways to Wander – Claire Hind and Clare Qualmann
54 intriguing ideas for different ways to take a walk – for enthusiasts, practitioners, students and academics

Walking's New Movement – Phil Smith
A tour-de-force about developments in walking and walk-performance for enthusiasts, practitioners, students and academics.

Desire Paths – Roy Bayfield
Designed to open your eyes to the landscape, and at the same time provide you with experimental walking exercises.

A Sardine Street Box of Tricks – Crab Man and Signpost
A guide for anyone making, or learning to make, walk-performances.

On Walking... and Stalking Sebald – Phil Smith
Describes a walk round Suffolk's lost villages, Cold War testing sites, black dogs, white deer and alien trails... and sets out a kind of walking for which the author is quietly famous. Walking that goes beyond the guidebook, behind the Tudor facade and beneath the blisters.

Nine Ways of Seeing a Body – Sandra Reeve
9 lenses through which the body can be viewed: object (Cartesian); subject (Grotowski); phenomenological (Husserl); somatic (Feldenkrais); contextual (self-reflection); interdependent (kinetic mirroring); environmental (Santiago theory); cultural (Csordas); ecological (Reeve).

Mythogeography – Phil Smith
The *fons et origo* of Phil Smith's writing about walking.

www.triarchypress.net/walking